Silicon Dreams

The Rise and Fall of Tech Titans

by

Dr. ant

Silicon Dreams: The Rise and Fall of Tech Titans

Contents

Introduction

The world of startups is a continuously evolving universe, constantly shaped by visionaries who dare to think differently and act boldly. It's a dynamic ecosystem where innovations aren't just encouraged—they're essential. This book seeks to explore this ever-changing landscape, delving into the factors that drive the tech industry and startup culture toward monumental success. Entrepreneurs, business students, and anyone fascinated by technology's relentless march will find a treasure trove of insights within these pages.

At its core, the tech startup ecosystem embodies a paradox: it's both chaotic and systematic, unpredictable yet governed by identifiable patterns. The turbulent journey from a mere idea to a fully-fledged company brimming with potential is one that many have embarked on, but not all have survived. Yet, it's precisely this blend of unpredictability and potential that fuels the spirit of innovation and cultivates an environment ripe for breakthrough ideas.

The very foundations of Silicon Valley rest on the stories of audacious thinkers and makers who weren't afraid to fail. What emerged as a small hub for technological ideas in California gradually became the epicenter of the tech universe. Entrepreneurs like Steve Jobs and Elon Musk set the stage by pushing boundaries and asking the question that every startup must courageously face: "What if?" Their narratives are intertwined with larger societal shifts that have consistently redefined what's possible in technology and business.

While many focus on the spectacular successes of startups that reached the zenith of industry fame, understanding the broader tapestry of the startup ecosystem requires examining a spectrum that includes both triumphant victories and spectacular failures. Learning from past crises and analyzing pivotal moments in tech history provide invaluable lessons for those walking the entrepreneurial path. The dot-com boom and bust, for example, serve as a powerful reminder of the fine line between visionary foresight and reckless ambition.

Startup culture, at its best, is an amalgamation of creativity and disruption. The explosion of ideas often starts humbly, in garages and college dorms, where intellect and creativity collide to give birth to groundbreaking concepts. These innovations are not just products of technological advancement but are deeply rooted in the culture they inhabit. The synergy between cultural evolution and technological progress propels startups forward, fostering an environment where failure is not only accepted but is viewed as a stepping stone towards success.

Navigating this landscape necessitates an understanding of not only the mechanics of business but the social dynamics that allow tech companies to thrive. The rise of social media platforms, e-commerce giants, and cloud computing services transformed industries and played crucial roles in the way businesses are structured today. For startups, grasping these shifts isn't just beneficial—it's essential for survival and growth.

In recent years, the surge of artificial intelligence, cryptocurrencies, and electric vehicles has added new dimensions to this ecosystem, presenting both unprecedented opportunities and unique challenges. The ethical implications of AI, the volatility of crypto markets, and the sustainability issues surrounding electric vehicles are topics that entrepreneurs must keenly watch and navigate with care. Success in the startup world demands a flexible mindset, willing to adapt and evolve with these emerging trends.

Central to any startup is the question of leadership. Visionary leaders steer their companies through uncharted waters, shaping not only their products but also their industries. The stories and strategies behind these leaders provide a blueprint for aspiring entrepreneurs. Equally important is the role of venture capital in fueling innovation. The financial backing of investors who recognize potential can transform an idea scribbled on a napkin into a reality that disrupts entire markets.

Yet, even as we celebrate the triumphs, it is crucial to remember the ongoing challenges, such as achieving gender equality in tech, safeguarding against cybersecurity threats, and handling the complex interplay of government regulations. Addressing these issues is not only vital for the equitable development of technology but also for inspiring the next generation of innovators to rise to the occasion and tackle tomorrow's problems with today's solutions.

This book calls on readers to think critically about what it takes to succeed in a world where technology and innovation are the driving forces. It seeks to demystify the startup phenomenon by revealing the highs and lows experienced by those at the forefront of this revolution. Aspiring entrepreneurs will find themselves challenged to envision beyond conventional limits, finding inspiration in the stories, lessons, and case studies that follow.

As we embark on this exploration, we invite you to consider not just the technical and business aspects of successful startups, but the human stories behind them—the passion, resilience, and unyielding spirit that defines this vibrant world. Prepare to be inspired, informed, and motivated as we unravel startup success in all its nuanced glory.

Chapter 1: Foundations of Silicon Valley

Take a moment to picture a dusty stretch of land in the mid-20th century, where a few visionaries began to lay the groundwork for what would become a global innovation powerhouse. Silicon Valley's rise didn't happen overnight—its reputation as a tech mecca was forged by a blend of relentless ambition, pioneering ideas, and a unique ethos that encouraged taking bold risks in pursuit of groundbreaking technological advancements. Back then, the industry was a fledgling notion, and the idea of turning silicon into something transformative was both a challenge and an opportunity seized by a handful of daring entrepreneurs. Key figures, such as William Shockley and the "Traitorous Eight," along with institutions like Stanford University, cultivated a fertile environment for creativity and disruption. Their contributions not only sparked early innovations in semiconductors but also set the tone for a collaborative culture that now defines the heart of tech entrepreneurship. Without the foundations they laid, the serendipity of innovation that characterizes Silicon Valley today might never have taken root.

The Birth of the Tech Industry

Silicon Valley as we know it today didn't emerge out of thin air; its roots can be traced back to a fascinating convergence of academic brilliance, wartime exigencies, and entrepreneurial spirit. The tech industry wasn't born overnight; it was birthed slowly, shaped by a series of strategic innovations and visionary individuals who laid its foundational stones. To truly understand the essence of Silicon Valley, one must look back to the fertile grounds of the mid-20th century, where the seeds of the tech revolution were sown.

Stanford University played a pivotal role in shaping what would become the beating heart of the tech industry. Under the visionary leadership of Frederick Terman, a former professor of electrical engineering, Stanford encouraged students not just to learn but to innovate. This ethos was revolutionary at the time. Terman, who would later become known as the "Father of Silicon Valley," foresaw the potential of harnessing the innovative spirit and turning academic insights into commercial successes. By nurturing a culture of experimentation and entrepreneurship, he laid the groundwork for a technological ecosystem that would thrive over the decades.

World War II had left its mark on the world, not just in geopolitical terms but also in technological advancements. The military's demand for advanced electronic devices to aid communication and surveillance led to increased investments in research and development. This period witnessed an unprecedented fusion of government, academia, and industry. It's crucial to recognize this triad as a springboard for numerous innovations, catalyzing the birth of tech endeavors that wouldn't have materialized otherwise.

The Bell Labs, famous for inventions like the transistor, played a significant role in this period. Though not situated in Silicon Valley, its innovations contributed directly to the valley's potential. The transistor, a vital component in modern electronics, is arguably one of the most groundbreaking inventions of that era. It made computers smaller, faster, and more reliable. The ripple effect of this innovation was profound, making digital technology viable for broader applications and easier commercialization for the entrepreneurial minded.

Amidst these technological advancements, a social and cultural shift was occurring in the region. There was a palpable spirit of rebellion against the traditional corporate culture. People dreamt of small ventures that could operate independently from larger bureaucratic enterprises. This aspiration gave rise to what could be described as an 'entrepreneurial counterculture,' a deviation from conventional norms that prioritized risk-taking and ingenuity. This ethos was reminiscent of the gold rush, where opportunities were abundant for those daring enough to seize them.

William Shockley, one of the co-inventors of the transistor, made a decision that would inadvertently kickstart a wave of technological entrepreneurship in Silicon Valley. When Shockley established Shockley Semiconductor Laboratory in Mountain View, it attracted some of the brightest minds in the field. However, dissatisfaction with his managerial approach led to the formation of Fairchild Semiconductor by eight of his employees, aptly nicknamed the "Traitorous Eight." Their departure marked the first of many 'spin-offs' that would become characteristic of the valley's culture, creating a domino effect as companies branched into new ventures, all rooted in a fertile ground of innovation.

Fairchild, in particular, deserves recognition for its pivotal role in creating the Silicon Valley we recognize today. It wasn't just a company; it became an incubator for talent and new ideas. From Fairchild's lineage sprang forth corporations like Intel, AMD, and many others, putting the area on the map as a growing tech hub. The company embodied a paradoxical blend of competition and collaboration, promoting a sense of community while fostering individual entrepreneurial ambitions. This delicate balance of shared knowledge and competitive edge became a defining characteristic of the emerging tech industry.

The military demand during the Cold War era also played a significant role in subsidizing the technological boom. Government contracts allowed startup companies to secure funding while taking risks on new technologies. This financial safety net provided a layer of confidence and stability that was necessary for trailblazing entrepreneurship. Moreover, the intertwined relationship between military needs and civilian applications ensured technology could seamlessly transition from defense to everyday use, catalyzing broader market acceptance.

As the silicon-based semiconductor began to dominate the market, the region's identity started to solidify. The term "Silicon Valley" itself draws from this period of semiconductor dominance. Unlike rolling out a specific product, this era was about laying critical infrastructure. The industry was no longer just crafting components; it was building the very general-purpose machines that would empower businesses and individuals alike.

This foundational era of the tech industry wasn't just about inventing lasting technologies but about sculpting an ethos that values innovation, risk, and the relentless pursuit of knowledge. This unique assembly of socio-economic factors and an unwavering commitment to technological advancements contributed to Silicon Valley's burgeoning influence. As we move forward in exploring the development of Silicon Valley, we'll see how these birth pangs shaped not just a region, but how they set the standard for technology-driven entrepreneurship across the globe. In subsequent chapters, we'll delve deeper into how these foundations were built upon, leading to an era of remarkable growth and transformation.

Key Players and Early Innovations

The early years of Silicon Valley were a time of immense creativity and remarkable visionaries who laid the groundwork for what would become the heart of the global tech industry. The term "Silicon Valley" itself is synonymous with a unique blend of entrepreneurship, innovation, and risk-taking that some of the world's most influential tech companies have emerged from. It all began with a handful of key players whose groundbreaking ideas and relentless pursuit of technological advancement set the stage for a revolution.

One cannot discuss the origins of Silicon Valley without mentioning the pivotal role of William Shockley, John Bardeen, and Walter Brattain. In the late 1940s, this trio of scientists, working at Bell Labs, invented the transistor. This tiny device, which could amplify and switch electronic signals, replaced vacuum tubes and became the fundamental building block of virtually all modern electronics. Their work earned them the Nobel Prize in Physics in 1956, but more importantly, it sparked the birth of the semiconductor industry.

Shockley, in particular, played a crucial role in Silicon Valley's development. He relocated to Palo Alto, California, and founded Shockley Semiconductor Laboratory in 1956. His contentious management style led to the defection of his top talent, who would famously go on to form Fairchild Semiconductor. This startup was to produce a cascade of innovations that catapulted Silicon Valley into a hub of tech entrepreneurship.

Fairchild Semiconductor's creation marked a turning point in Silicon Valley. Known for producing high-quality silicon wafers, the company rapidly gained recognition for its advancements in integrated circuit technology. Founded by the so-called "Traitorous Eight," these former Shockley employees—Gordon Moore, Robert Noyce, and others—injected vitality and competition into the burgeoning tech scene. The legacy of Fairchild Semiconductor was more than its products; it was a training ground for future legends of the industry, contributing knowledge, capital, and culture to subsequent pioneering firms.

Among these legends were Gordon Moore and Robert Noyce themselves, who would later co-found Intel Corporation in 1968. Intel's development of the microprocessor further solidified Silicon Valley's position at the forefront of technological innovation. The microprocessor's influence cannot be overstated, as it revolutionized computing by miniaturizing what used to be room-sized mainframes into desktop computers, eventually making personal computing accessible to the masses.

Another monumental figure in Silicon Valley's early days was Steve Jobs, co-founder of Apple Inc. Despite not being the progenitor of the tech industry in Silicon Valley, Jobs' vision and charisma turned Apple into a synonym for design elegance and user-friendly technology. With products like the Apple II and Macintosh, Apple demonstrated the potential of personal computing in everyday life, inspiring a generation of entrepreneurs and redefining consumer technology.

Silicon Valley's early success wasn't just a product of technological innovation, but also the interplay of academia and industry. Stanford University's proximity played an undeniable role, providing both a stream of talented graduates and a steady flow of groundbreaking research. Stanford's encouragement of entrepreneurial endeavors allowed for seamless collaboration between academic research and commercial application, creating a unique ecosystem conducive to innovation.

The culture of risk and reward fostered by these early pioneers attracted not just engineers and scientists, but also the investment community. The region's density of venture capitalists keen to fund bold ventures helped to transform ambitious ideas into billion-dollar realities. This interplay of academic excellence, industry foresight, and investment potential nurtured a uniquely dynamic environment, setting the stage for Silicon Valley to explode into a global epicenter for technology and innovation.

It wasn't just the technology that made these players key to Silicon Valley's narrative; it was their willingness to take risks and challenge the status quo. They weren't just creating new products but were envisioning new paradigms of what was possible. These men and women were not satisfied with simply improving existing technologies; they endeavored to redefine them entirely. Their quest for innovation wasn't driven solely by profit but by a genuine desire to push the boundaries of human capability through technology.

The inventive spirit that these early players embodied laid the foundation for a continuous cycle of innovation that Silicon Valley is known for today. From Shockley's transistor to Jobs' innovative Apple designs, each milestone served as a catalyst for further advancements, paving the way for future generations to walk in their footsteps with a shared sense of possibility. A shared ethos of creativity, determination, and often contentious collaboration pushed the limits that society set for itself, cementing the region's status as the bedrock of global technological advancement.

Innovation wasn't limited to engineering feats; early Silicon Valley also marked the beginning of revolutionary business practices. The region saw the evolution of corporate structures, stock options, and a casual workplace culture that valued merit over hierarchy. This was a place where a scientist could become a CEO, embodying a culture of equality and the belief that anyone could rise through sheer innovation and impact, regardless of their background.

These foundational elements provided the backdrop for the dramatic expansion and diversification of technology industries in subsequent decades. From semiconductors to software, and eventually the internet, these key players and their innovations set in motion a transformation that extended far beyond the geographical area. Silicon Valley's ethos has permeated global business practices, inspiring countless other tech hubs around the world to adopt a similar blend of creativity, investment, and entrepreneurship.

As we reflect on these pioneering individuals and the early innovations of Silicon Valley, it becomes clear that the fabric of the tech universe was woven from countless threads of vision, tenacity, and collaboration. They've transformed what began as a sleepy agricultural region into a bustling nucleus of technological advancement. Future chapters in this story will continue to build on this foundation, just as the current generation of entrepreneurs is driven by the giants whose shoulders they stand on.

Chapter 2: The Dot-Com Boom

In the mid-1990s, the internet wasn't just a burgeoning frontier; it was a gold rush, a dazzling intersection of opportunity and ambition that reshaped the global economy. The promise of digital riches lured scores of investors and dreamers, sparking a frenetic wave of tech startups, each vying to leave its mark on this new digital landscape. Valuations soared to dizzying heights as venture capitalists poured money into any company with a ".com" domain. The traditional rules of business were upended, as growth metrics replaced profitability in the race for market supremacy. Yet, this exuberant expansion couldn't last forever. By the early 2000s, the bubble burst, leaving behind a trail of defunct companies and shattered illusions. The ensuing economic fallout served as a stark reminder of the industry's volatility and the perils of unchecked speculation. Despite the collapse, the dot-com boom planted seeds of innovation, laying the groundwork for the tech giants that would eventually rise from its ashes. Entrepreneurs today can glean invaluable lessons from this era, understanding both the intoxicating lure of rapid growth and the critical importance of sustainable business practices.

Surging Investments and Sky-High Valuations

The late 1990s were a whirlwind of excitement and optimism. Investors, buoyed by the promise of the internet, were pouring unprecedented amounts of money into tech startups, hoping to capitalize on the digital frontier. Entrepreneurs, many fresh out of college or dropping out in pursuit of the next big thing, felt they were on the cusp of a new era. It was a time when the belief in the transformative power of technology sidestepped traditional business metrics. The 'dot-com' suffix became synonymous with potential and possibility, irrespective of business models, often leading to company valuations that made traditional investors scratch their heads in disbelief.

In this heady atmosphere, venture capitalists played a pivotal role. Flush with funds from a wide array of sources, they became the fairy godparents of Silicon Valley, wielding the power to breathe life into the ambitious ideas of eager entrepreneurs. The typical venture capital rhythm of investment rounds was replaced by a frenetic pace; money was dished out in millions, sometimes with little more than a compelling pitch deck. All for a chance to invest in the next big dot-com success story — a platform that could redefine how we shopped, communicated, or searched for information.

These investments weren't just sizeable; they were transformative. Skilled developers soon became some of the most sought-after professionals. Office spaces transformed into playful hubs of creativity, embodying the culture of innovation and freedom. The atmosphere was one where conventional rules were rewritten. The idea of twenty-year-old CEOs commanding billion-dollar companies didn't just seem plausible—it became a badge of honor for the iconoclasts disrupting traditional industries.

As the investments surged, so did the valuations. Companies with virtually no revenue were hitting the stock market with IPOs, often seeing stock prices soar on the first day of trading. This created a feedback loop of investment euphoria: more investment drove higher valuations, which, in turn, attracted yet more investment. This cycle perpetuated the perception that profits were secondary to growth, which was assumed to be virtually limitless in the online realm.

But why were these valuations skyrocketing? The late 1990s was a period when the internet was still novel to the general public and wildly misunderstood by much of the traditional finance community. It promised a transformation of unprecedented scale, throwing open markets ready for disruption. While some had doubts, many believed in the market's boundless prospects. Analysts frequently used unique metrics paired with upbeat projections, often extrapolating futuristic growth scenarios in a world where innovation was king.

Take, for example, the valuation of companies like Pets.com, which became emblematic of this boom. With a catchy puppet mascot and ads during the Super Bowl, Pets.com quickly gained national recognition. But even with its public success, the underlying business model was shaky—something both investors and the public would later learn the hard way. Meanwhile, companies like Amazon began their journeys as small dot-com ventures, surviving the hype and demonstrating sustainable growth beyond mere valuation spikes.

This surreal landscape was heavily populated by stories of overnight millionaires. Employees took stock options in lieu of salaries, betting on their companies' future success. For many, it was worth the gamble, as their companies' stocks surged beyond any rational expectation. It wasn't uncommon for these young employees to find themselves millionaires after an IPO, working at companies with exuberant, lofty valuations.

The mood was infectious, spreading beyond Silicon Valley and affecting markets worldwide as hope and greed played tug-of-war. Wall Street, traditionally skeptical of startups, was charmed by stories of disruption and visionary CEOs. The initial public offerings of tech companies were turning into cultural events, often overshadowed by the opening numbers and heralded by journalists as dawns of new ages. Across the spectrum, people bought into the narrative of technological utopia on the doorstep, often sidelining standard practices of due diligence and skepticism.

Such dizzying valuations weren't only fueled by speculation but by a new economy's promise—a paradigm where old rules seemed obsolete. It was about what could be, rather than what was. This mindset facilitated an environment where business plans sketched on a napkin at a coffee shop could manifest into multinational corporations in the digital space—the ultimate proof, for some, was in radical disruption rather than methodical planning.

As the clock ticked towards the millennium, few stopped to question if investing patterns were sustainable or if perhaps the valuations were too good to last. Instead, it felt like a characteristic of a new world bubbling into view, an economic storyline eagerly pursued in mainstream narratives. The new decade brimmed with hope, blinded by an expectation that digital transformation would bring untold prosperity, bypassing the cyclical constraints of traditional business cycles.

Yet, surging investments and sky-high valuations inevitably carried a set of inherent risks. As with any gold rush, there were underlying instabilities and assumptions left unquestioned, often buried beneath the layers of enthusiasm for change. But at the height of the dot-com boom, doubt was a scarce commodity, almost as rare as caution. Resting on a fragile balance between hype and hope, the stage was set for a dramatic climax.

Reflecting on the period offers invaluable lessons for today's entrepreneurs and investors. The dot-com boom was more than a chapter in history—it was a reminder of the challenge to balance visionary ambition with grounded realism. It highlighted the importance of understanding both technological potential and market fundamentals, urging today's innovators to embrace robust business models alongside dreaming big. For those looking to navigate today's startup landscape, the dot-com era continues to serve as a story of caution and inspiration—a dream realized for a moment, before the rules of economics called it to account.

The Burst and Economic Fallout

The end of the 1990s marked a seismic shift in the economic landscape, a time of both troubling despair and hard-earned lessons. The dot-com bubble, which had rapidly inflated due to unfettered excitement and speculation, burst with devastating force. Many startups, once seen as sure bets to deliver unprecedented wealth, found themselves teetering on the brink of disaster. The fallout wasn't just a wake-up call for the tech industry; it was a moment that reshaped how investors, entrepreneurs, and policymakers approached future innovations.

The initial catalyst for this economic upheaval was an undeniable exuberance, bordering on irrational, for the limitless potential the internet promised. Investors, flush with cash and driven by the lure of technological utopia, poured money into internet companies with little regard for sustainable business models. E-commerce was exploding, web portals were cropping up daily, and consumer behavior was rapidly shifting towards online modes of interaction. But behind this thin, glittering veneer, many companies were hemorrhaging cash faster than they could generate revenue.

As stock prices soared to astronomical heights, the eventual burst became inevitable. It was an implosion of valuations that had less to do with technology itself and more to do with the dangerous cocktail of hype and neglect of fundamental business principles. Technology startups that had once been media darlings found their valuations plummeting overnight. Companies that appeared invincible were declared insolvent within weeks, their business models scrutinized and often found wanting.

For entrepreneurs, the collapse was both humbling and instructive. It revealed the importance of establishing a strong value proposition and the need to balance visionary thinking with financial sensibility. Some viewed the crash as a crucible through which only viable, innovative companies emerged stronger and more resilient. Amazon, for instance, weathered the storm by maintaining a focus on customer satisfaction and operational efficiency. Others weren't as lucky.

Investors learned to be more discerning, keenly aware that startups required more than just a tempting idea to succeed—they needed viable business models and realistic timelines for profitability. The wave of bankruptcies forced venture capitalists to recalibrate their approach to funding, prioritizing governance and due diligence over gut feelings. These shifts in attitude would serve as the foundation for a more balanced investment strategy in the following years.

The broader economic consequences of the burst extended well beyond Silicon Valley. Stock market indices tanked, affecting not just tech stocks but also impacting pension funds, individual retirement accounts, and corporate investments. The United States economy, and indeed the global economy, experienced a tangible slowdown as financial institutions grappled with significant losses.

Job markets, particularly within the tech industry, suffered as layoffs became unavoidable. Thousands of tech workers faced unemployment, and firms that once paid exorbitantly for talent were forced to cut salaries or offer stock options that were now worthless. These challenging times were marked not only by fiscal austerity but also by an introspection that prompted many to rethink their careers, leading to a wave of innovation in unexpected areas.

However, from the ashes of failed enterprises rose a renewed sense of prudence and understanding. Startups, once fixated on rapid growth at any cost, began to value sustainability. The concept of "lean startup," popularized later, can trace its philosophical roots back to this period of recalibration. Entrepreneurs focused on creating minimum viable products, iterating based on customer feedback, and achieving profitability before scaling massively.

From an educational perspective, business schools quickly adapted their curricula to include case studies from the dot-com crash. The objective was to equip future entrepreneurs with a balanced perspective—cheering them on to innovate while tempering their expectations with real-world financial constraints. The lessons learned during this period were not just about avoiding similar pitfalls but also about recognizing the signs of speculative bubbles early enough to mitigate risks.

For policymakers, the burst highlighted the necessity of prudent regulatory frameworks that could ensure market stability without stifling innovation. Various legislative bodies across the world took heed, crafting policies to safeguard against another unchecked speculative spree. While too much regulation can stifle innovation, an appropriate balance was sought to cultivate sustainable technological advancement.

The burst also served as a storytelling moment, a shared experience for those who lived through it. It was a time when liquid dreams congealed into hard realities, instructing those moving forward to blend big-picture visions with down-to-earth practicality. Many entrepreneurs who survived the crash emerged with renewed vigor, equipped with insider knowledge that was both scar tissue and a badge of honor.

As with any great upheaval, the dot-com crash was a period of both reckoning and reinvention. While the immediate impact was undeniably severe, its long-term consequences became gateways for growth, compelling the tech industry to evolve robustly. When the tide eventually receded, what remained were the gems of innovation—startups committed to enduring principles, investors with tempered optimism, and entrepreneurs ready to turn lessons learned into future successes.

In hindsight, the burst and its economic fallout were both humbling and illuminating—a testament to the resilience of human ingenuity in overcoming adversity. This period taught the world that while ambition is the fuel for innovation, it's the grounding in reality that steers it toward success. The narrative continues as an indelible chapter in the ongoing saga of technology and enterprise, a potent reminder that even in the face of collapse, there's immense opportunity for those willing to learn and adapt.

Chapter 3: Startup Culture and Innovation

In the pulsating heart of startup culture, innovation isn't just encouraged—it's imperative. Startup environments thrive on a potent cocktail of audacity and ingenuity that propels nascent ideas toward transformative disruptions. This culture is often characterized by a "garage band mentality," where creativity takes precedence over hierarchy, and risk is embraced rather than feared. Founders instill a shared vision among their passionate teams, fostering an atmosphere where unconventional thinking is not just welcomed but is the norm. The spirit of disruption fuels these dynamic spaces, where yesterday's failings provide the critical lessons that shape tomorrow's triumphs. Aspiring entrepreneurs dive headlong into challenges, armed with a relentless drive to redefine markets and pioneer new paradigms. This relentless pursuit of the next big thing is what keeps startup culture perpetually vibrant and at the forefront of the tech industry.

The Garage Band Mentality

In the world of startup culture, there's a unique and captivating ethos often dubbed the "Garage Band Mentality." This concept isn't just a nod to the humble beginnings that mark many a tech giant story, but it's a deep-seated mindset that propels innovation and creativity. It's about tapping into the unbridled passion, raw energy, and sheer determination found in a group of musicians practicing in their parent's garage. Translated to the business world, it's the idea that a small, nimble team with limited resources can disrupt industries much like a band can move a generation of fans with a homemade album.

This mentality thrives on the audacity to dream big despite humble beginnings. It draws inspiration from tales like that of Hewlett-Packard starting in a Palo Alto garage, providing a guiding myth for the Silicon Valley narrative. But this approach isn't about nostalgia; it's a strategic mindset grounded in being lean and agile. It's about making do with what you have and focusing on the essentials—innovation and a killer instinct to break through the noise.

For entrepreneurs, embracing the garage band mentality means nurturing a culture where everyone's role is significant, where titles and hierarchies dissolve in the pursuit of a shared goal. When a startup is at its nascent stage, every member is as valuable as the next—each brings a unique skill set that complements others, forming a cohesive unit much like a band. The CEO might double as the janitor, and the software developer could lead product design discussions. It's an all-hands-on-deck approach that fosters a collective ownership of both challenges and victories.

Moreover, this mentality encourages experimentation and tolerates failure. The garage is not just a physical space; it's a mental one that allows for the freedom to try new things without the paralyzing fear of failure. Just as musicians experiment with different sounds to create something new, entrepreneurs in a startup experiment with different strategies and products. They deploy the "fail fast" philosophy—quickly testing ideas, learning from errors, and iterating—rather than spending months perfecting a single concept that might not work in the end.

The garage band mentality also implies a sense of scrappiness, a willingness to cut through bureaucracy. Without the weight of established processes and systems that can slow innovation, startups can move faster, much like a garage band can produce and distribute music without a record label's approval. This nimbleness is key, as speed can be a significant advantage over larger, less agile competitors.

A critical aspect of this approach is maintaining a hungry mindset. Even as a startup grows and gains success, preserving that initial hustle is vital. Complacency can be the kryptonite of innovation. The passion that ignited the idea in the garage must evolve but never extinguish. It's about continuously seeking out new challenges, staying curious, and always pushing the boundaries. The garage band mentality is flexible and evolves with the startup, adapting to new circumstances while maintaining its core spirit.

However, this mindset doesn't come without its challenges. The very lack of structure that empowers creativity can also lead to chaos. Entrepreneurs must know when to introduce some level of formality and discipline without stifling that innovative spirit. As the startup scales, the challenge becomes balancing the creative chaos with the needs of an expanding organization requiring order and reliability.

Additionally, embracing this mentality might also mean accepting the impermanence of roles and team compositions. As with garage bands, which can see fluctuating members and evolving sounds, startups may find that the team that starts the journey might look different from the one that achieves the ultimate goal. It's a natural progression, reinforcing the need to adapt and change as the venture grows.

Ultimately, the garage band mentality in startup culture isn't just a romantic notion; it's a practical framework for achieving innovation and success. This approach gives struggling entrepreneurs hope, proving that you don't need a massive budget or a sprawling office to make a significant impact. You need determination, an open mind to risk, and a relentless drive to push the creative envelope. It's a reminder that significant change often starts in the most unassuming places, much like a revolution can start from the simple strumming of a guitar in a garage.

Fostering Creativity and Disruption

The spirit of creativity and disruption sits at the heart of every successful startup culture. As we delve deeper into the tech industry, it's clear that innovation doesn't just happen; it's fostered. The word 'foster' itself implies nurturing, providing a space where ideas can grow, be challenged, and ultimately, thrive. This section explores what it means to foster creativity and disruption in the context of startup culture and why these elements are critical for success.

Startups, by their very nature, are all about challenging the status quo. They don't just seek efficiency; they aim to rewrite the rulebook entirely. Think of companies like Airbnb or Uber, which transformed their respective industries not by improving existing models but by disrupting them entirely. Disruption stems from a captivating mix of creativity, boldness, and a willingness to take risks. It requires an environment where unconventional thinking is not only accepted, but actively encouraged.

Creating such an environment requires more than just physical space; it demands a cultural mindset. In Silicon Valley, this mindset has been famously captured by the "fail fast, fail often" philosophy. However, it's not just about the willingness to fail. At its core lies an implicit understanding that each failure is a stepping-stone toward a novel solution or an innovative approach that hasn't been considered before. This is key for startups where the road to success is often paved with setbacks and iterations.

One tactic that fosters this environment is the cross-pollination of ideas through diverse teams. Diversity in backgrounds, experiences, and perspectives can lead to surprisingly innovative solutions to complex problems. As research has shown, diverse teams often outperform homogeneous ones in creative tasks because they bring different viewpoints and challenge each other's thinking. The clash of ideas that arises from diversity can be a powerful catalyst for creativity and, ultimately, disruption.

Consider hackathons or innovation jams, where bright minds come together for a brief but intense period to solve problems. These gatherings epitomize the creative and disruptive culture found in startups. By encouraging rapid prototyping and immediate feedback, they provide a fertile ground for creativity to flourish. Moreover, they showcase how constraints, such as time limits, can paradoxically fuel creativity by forcing swift decision-making and prioritization.

While nurturing internal creativity is essential, startups often look outwards for inspiration and potential collaboration. Open innovation—where companies share ideas and collaborate with external partners—can lead to faster and more diverse avenues for development. By engaging with the broader ecosystem, whether it's through partnerships, open-source projects, or innovation labs, startups can expand their horizons and leverage external expertise and resources to drive disruption.

Nevertheless, fostering creativity and disruption isn't without its challenges. One major hurdle is the potential for creative burnout. Breaking new ground constantly demands intense intellectual and emotional effort, which can lead to fatigue over time. It's crucial for entrepreneurs and startup leaders to recognize this risk and cultivate a supportive atmosphere that prioritizes well-being alongside innovation. This might involve flexible working options, opportunities for rest, and encouragement to pursue passion projects.

The process of fostering creativity and disruption must also guard against the creeping influence of rigidity as companies grow. As startups scale, the structures and processes that come with size can stifle the very creativity that led to their initial success. To counter this, some companies adopt strategies like maintaining small, autonomous teams that work on distinct projects, effectively creating a "company within a company." This approach helps replicate the creative dynamism of the startup phase while benefiting from the resources of a larger organization.

Leadership plays a pivotal role in this cultural transformation. Visionary leaders such as Steve Jobs or Elon Musk are often credited with cultivating environments where innovation thrives. Their ability to articulate a compelling vision and instill a culture that values curiosity and bold thinking is paramount. Yet, not every leader needs to be larger than life. Sometimes the quieter, facilitative leadership that empowers team members to take initiative and own their projects can be equally effective in maintaining an innovative culture.

Encouraging creativity isn't just about grand gestures or groundbreaking products. Sometimes, it's about celebrating the small wins and iterative gains that build over time into significant breakthroughs. Startup cultures that emphasize continuous learning and adaptability often find themselves at the forefront of disruption. This mindset allows them to pivot when necessary, seize new opportunities, and innovate faster than larger corporations that may be weighed down by bureaucracy.

In today's fast-paced digital economy, the ability to foster creativity and disruption is an invaluable asset for any startup. It requires a strategic blend of culture, leadership, and process. But more importantly, it calls for an unwavering belief in the power of ideas to change the world. As we continue to observe the rise and fall of ventures in the tech realm, one thing remains certain: those who embrace and cultivate creativity and disruption will be the ones leading us into the future.

Chapter 4: Icons of Innovation

In the ever-evolving landscape of technology, certain figures stand as towering icons, reshaping the very fabric of modern society with their visionary prowess and unyielding perseverance. At the heart of this transformative journey is Steve Jobs, whose relentless dedication to design and user experience propelled Apple from a fledgling startup to a global powerhouse, embedding innovation into the company's DNA. Similarly, the founders of Google, Larry Page and Sergey Brin, harnessed the power of data and algorithms to redefine how we access information, transforming our inquisitive queries into seamless digital interactions. These pioneers did more than build companies; they carved out new paradigms, inspiring legions of entrepreneurs to dream bigger and bolder. Their stories epitomize the spirit of innovation, proving that with the right blend of creativity, risk-taking, and resilience, the unthinkable becomes possible. Through their enduring legacies, they offer invaluable lessons to those who dare to challenge the status quo and sculpt the future.

The Journey of Apple and Steve Jobs

Apple and Steve Jobs stand synonymous with innovation, ambition, and relentless pursuit of perfection. Far from the archetype of most tech giants, their journey began from a small garage in Cupertino, California. In this modest setting, Jobs, along with Steve Wozniak and the lesser-known but crucial Ronald Wayne, laid the foundations of what would become a revolutionary force in personal computing.

From the very start, Apple's products didn't just aim to meet market needs but to redefine them. The debut of the Apple I in 1976 was a groundbreaking moment, establishing a new benchmark for accessible technology. It was soon followed by the more sophisticated Apple II, which brought color graphics to the masses. The success of these early products was instrumental in Apple's initial rise, propelled by Jobs' vision for sleek design and user-friendly interfaces. However, it was not a journey without its hurdles.

By the mid-1980s, Apple was facing internal discord, and Jobs found himself at odds with then-CEO John Sculley. This tension led to Jobs' ouster in 1985. Although a setback, his departure opened new avenues; he founded NeXT and acquired Pixar, steamrolling pathways in both software development and digital animation. This period away from Apple wasn't a break but rather an incubation of ideas and growth that enriched Jobs' perspective on leadership and innovation.

Jobs' eventual return to Apple in 1997 marked the beginning of a renaissance for the company. Facing financial and creative decline, his leadership resurrected Apple's standing in the tech world. His strategic focus wasn't just limited to hardware but extended to integrating software and hardware for an unparalleled user experience. The introduction of the iMac redefined aesthetics, but it was the launch of the iPod in 2001 that acted as a game-changer, not just for Apple but for the music industry at large.

The narrative of Apple and Steve Jobs isn't just about inventing successful products; it's an exploration of a paradigm shift in thinking. Jobs believed that technology could become an extension of human expression, a belief that moved beyond the development of gadgets to the creation of the iTunes Store and later the App Store. These platforms didn't just solidify Apple's innovative reputation but also reshaped entire industries. Digital music, once rampant with piracy, found new life, marked by convenient, legal downloads.

Apple's journey reflects a commitment to a core philosophy: the intersection of art and technology. Jobs emphasized this blend through Apple's clean product lines and intuitive designs. The release of the iPhone in 2007 cemented Apple as a leader in innovation, integrating communication, entertainment, and computing into one handheld device. The lure of such seamless integration captivated consumers and competitors alike, sparking the smartphone race that's still in motion today.

However, the path was peppered with challenges. Compelling designs and revolutionary ideas had to be balanced with practicality and market acceptance. The release of the iPad pushed boundaries further, innovating how we consume media and manage daily tasks. Despite skepticism from those clinging to desktops and laptops, the iPad initiated a new trend towards portable computing solutions.

Jobs' leadership style was as much a part of Apple's story as the products themselves. Often described as demanding and sometimes harsh, his insistence on excellence pushed the company to unprecedented heights. The balance he struck between micro-managing details and trusting his teams' creative instincts resulted in products that resonated deeply with consumers worldwide. This dynamic spoke directly to leaders and entrepreneurs about maintaining vision while fostering innovation.

Through the ups and downs, Jobs maintained a central vision that extended beyond mere consumerism: empowering individuals through beautifully crafted, intuitive technology. This vision inspired a cult-like following, a community rather than just a customer base, which continues to drive Apple's success long after Jobs' passing in 2011.

The journey of Apple and Steve Jobs is a compelling chronicle of resilience, risk, and, ultimately, triumph. It speaks volumes about the power of marrying vision with execution, a lesson for entrepreneurs and industry veterans alike. It reminds us that success isn't just about having a great idea but about cultivating a culture of innovation and challenging the status quo.

For those inspired by Apple's ascent and Steve Jobs' legacy, their story is a testament to the power of passion, the importance of adaption, and the relentless quest for excellence. As we continue exploring new frontiers in technology, the principles that drove Apple's success remain as relevant as ever—not confined to any single era or industry, they serve as guiding stars for innovators around the globe.

Google's Vision and Growth

To talk about Google is to explore a story of relentless ambition, creativity, and influence that reshaped how we interact with information. When Sergey Brin and Larry Page conceived Google in a Stanford University dorm room, they weren't just crafting a search engine; they were attempting to categorize the vast array of information scattered across the internet. The vision was audacious: to make the world's information universally accessible and useful. It's a goal that, decades later, continues to drive the company's evolution.

Initially, the project was called "Backrub," a nod to its ability to analyze the "backlinks" pointing to a given webpage. This method promised better search results by mimicking the way academic papers are judged by the quality and quantity of citations. As the algorithm matured, it became apparent that Brin and Page were onto something potentially groundbreaking. In 1998, they officially launched Google, a name that would soon become synonymous with internet search.

In its early years, Google operated differently from its competitors. It utilized a clean, uncluttered homepage with its logo and a search bar right at the center. Most search engines of that era were packed with news, ads, and various hyperlinks, attempting to be portals to the web. Google redefined this standard by providing a simple, fast, and efficient search experience that won users over quickly, planting the first seeds of its rapid growth.

As Google's user base blossomed, so did Brin and Page's vision for the company. It wasn't just about providing better search results; it was about making data retrieval seamless across all formats and devices. They began developing services like Gmail, Google Maps, and Google News, each product a testament to their mission of categorizing and improving access to information.

One of Google's most significant steps in diversifying and growing its business came with the development of the Android operating system.

Acquiring Android Inc. in 2005 marked Google's strategic expansion into mobile technology, setting the stage for the smartphone revolution. Despite heavy competition, Android became a leader in the mobile OS market. Its success exemplifies Google's broader strategy of placing its software platforms—and thereby its search and ads—at the core of users' digital lives.

Key to Google's strategy was embracing an innovative corporate culture that encouraged risk-taking and experimentation. This ethos not only attracted top talent but also maintained a steady flow of groundbreaking products. "20% Time," an initiative that allowed employees to dedicate a fifth of their workweek to projects outside their job description, was instrumental in nurturing creativity, leading to innovations like Gmail and Google News.

Google's growth wasn't just due to its technical prowess or innovative products; it was driven by a business model built around advertising. Google's AdWords and AdSense redefined online advertising by enabling businesses to target ads directly to user interests on a scale that had never been done before. This shift not only provided a critical revenue stream but allowed Google to offer its products free of charge, further increasing its user base.

While Google's ascent was meteoric, it wasn't without obstacles. The company faced regulatory scrutiny on a global scale, necessitating a constant pivot and strategic maneuvering. Challenges ranging from concerns over monopoly power to data privacy regulations forced Google to adapt. How a company manages growth in light of these obstacles is a testament to its resilience and vision.

Today, as part of the Alphabet conglomerate, Google operates at the forefront of many cutting-edge technologies, including artificial intelligence, machine learning, and quantum computing. Each new area of focus reflects their vision of future innovation and growth. The ethos of 'moonshot thinking'—the aim to solve massive problems with radical solutions—encourages Google to remain an icon of innovation.

The journey of Google is more than the tale of a start-up turned corporate giant; it's a narrative about the power of a clear vision complemented by strategic growth. Aspiring entrepreneurs and business leaders can find endless lessons in how Google balanced ambition with practical execution. As it continues to influence global technology standards, Google's ongoing commitment to explore the boundaries of what's possible reminds us of the transformative power of innovation when combined with robust vision and unwavering ambition.

Chapter 5: Social Media Revolution

The advent of social media marked a pivotal shift in how businesses and individuals communicate, transforming relationships and reshaping industries in the process. This revolution ignited a tidal wave of connectivity, as platforms like Facebook emerged from dorm room dreams to global prominence, redefining the way we share, socialize, and sell. Entrepreneurs quickly realized that the digital forum offered unprecedented access to consumers, while brand narratives could now unfold in real-time across virtual communities. Twitter joined the fray, offering a new channel for instant updates and public discourse, yet constantly grappling with the challenges of miscommunication and moderation. As these platforms evolved, so too did the strategies businesses employed, learning to navigate algorithms and engagement metrics to capture attention in an increasingly fragmented digital landscape. Far from a mere trend, the rise of social media represents a fundamental revolution in both marketing and consumer behavior, offering lessons in adaptability and innovation essential to any entrepreneur aiming for success in today's tech-driven marketplace.

Facebook's Rise to Dominance

In the vast chronicle of social media's ascendancy, Facebook's story is
nothing short of legendary. Starting in a college dorm room at Harvard
University, this digital behemoth reshaped how humans connect globally.
It wasn't just the technology that distinguished Facebook, but how Mark
Zuckerberg, along with his co-founders, harnessed the very essence of
connectivity to create an unprecedented online community. Many startups
attempted to create social networks, yet Facebook's meteoric rise was
driven by a keen understanding of human psychology and an unrelenting
pursuit of scale.

At its core, Facebook connected users through a simple interface,
facilitating interaction like no other platform at the time. But what set it
apart were the innovative dynamics that allowed users to share life's
moments at the click of a button. This wasn't just a digital space to curate
an online persona; it was a living, breathing community designed to
replicate social experiences.

Facebook's growth wasn't serendipitous; it was meticulously planned.
Critical to its initial success was the exclusivity granted to Ivy League
students, creating a sense of prestige and allure. As Facebook slowly
expanded to other educational institutions, the network effect took root,
and soon after, there was no stopping its growth trajectory. From an
exclusive club, it transformed into a ubiquitous platform that transcended
borders and cultures.

The platform's adaptability was another cornerstone of its rise. While
maintaining a core identity, Facebook continually evolved its features to
stay relevant and engaging. The introduction of the News Feed
revolutionized how users consumed content—a stream of information that
mirrored social interactions and kept users coming back for more. This
relentless innovation was underpinned by a deep well of user data,
allowing Facebook to refine its offerings with surgical precision.

Advertising became Facebook's financial lifeline, redefining the digital marketing landscape. The genius was in its ability to offer highly targeted ads utilizing the treasure trove of user data it amassed. Advertisers could now pinpoint their audience with previously unimaginable accuracy, seamlessly integrating commerce with social interaction. For entrepreneurs and businesses, this was a game-changer. It offered unparalleled tools to reach and engage customers, setting a new standard in commercial advertising.

Scaling wasn't just about more users but fostering a vibrant ecosystem of developers and businesses. Through its API, Facebook opened its platform to third-party developers, spawning a myriad of applications that enhanced user experience and brought additional layers of functionality. This ecosystem fostered an unprecedented level of innovation and engagement, creating symbiotic relationships that spurred further growth.

Yet, with great power came great scrutiny. Facebook's rise was not without challenges. Issues surrounding privacy and data security turned the spotlight on the behemoth, raising questions about the ethics of its practices. There were debates about the extent of its influence on public opinion, governance, and even democratic institutions. These challenges heralded a new era of accountability, forcing Facebook to pivot and adjust in the face of global pressure.

Nonetheless, Facebook held a unique position among its peers. Its ability to not only survive but thrive amid adversity was a testament to its resilience and strategic foresight. The company focused on diversification, acquiring Instagram and WhatsApp, cementing its dominance across different demographics and use cases. These strategic acquisitions ensured that Facebook remained a robust force within the digital realm, fortifying its position against rising competitors.

The drive towards expansion also involved a dedication to technology and innovation. Initiatives like Facebook's artificial intelligence research lab signify the company's commitment to staying at the forefront of technological advances. These cutting-edge developments hinted not just at maintaining relevance, but actively shaping the future of global communication.

Ultimately, Facebook's journey from a collegiate project to a global titan offers invaluable lessons for entrepreneurs and business students. The company showcased the potency of product-market fit, the importance of continuous evolution, and the impact of strategic thinking in achieving sustained growth. It taught us that while invention can spark attention, innovation, and adaptability fuel lasting success.

For those enamored by startup culture and tech innovations, Facebook's rise is both an inspiration and a warning. The balance of growth with responsibility, and the foresight to anticipate both opportunities and challenges, are crucial in navigating the turbulent seas of tech entrepreneurship. Facebook's story is a compelling narrative of ambition, strategy, and transformation that continues to influence the digital landscape and inspire future innovators.

Twitter's Role and Challenges

Within the rapidly transforming landscape of digital communication, Twitter has carved out a unique space. Unlike its social media counterparts, which emphasize visual content or close-knit communities, Twitter excels at real-time dialogue and information dissemination. It's gained recognition as a powerful tool that amplifies voices globally, but not without facing a myriad of challenges along the way.

Twitter's inception was a response to a developing need for instantaneous exchange of ideas and news. Initially, its appeal lay in its simplicity—a platform for succinct interactions. Limiting messages to 140 characters meant Twitter fostered brevity, encouraging users to be concise and direct. The challenges associated with such brevity included the difficulty of conveying complex ideas in such a limited space, yet that constraint became its hallmark, promoting creativity and rapid engagement. The question is, how does a platform expand and continue to engage users without losing the essence of its original appeal?

The platform's role in fostering social change and disseminating information quickly became apparent during pivotal events such as the Arab Spring. Twitter allowed people to coordinate efforts, share immediate accounts of protests, and, significantly, bypass traditional media channels. This ability to provide unfiltered perspectives on worldwide events raised Twitter to a level of unforeseen importance. However, this amplified voice brought scrutiny, especially regarding how information is managed and verified on such an unrestricted platform.

One of the primary challenges Twitter has faced is managing misinformation. Given its model relies on user-generated content that spreads almost instantaneously, differentiating factual information from misleading narratives has become an arduous task. Twitter has employed various strategies, such as partnering with fact-checking organizations and employing algorithms to detect suspect material. Yet, these steps haven't fully eradicated the problem, and debates continue over what role, if any, Twitter should play in moderating content while adhering to principles of free speech.

Moreover, Twitter's open nature has led to challenges concerning user safety and harassment. The platform's commitment to free dialogue sometimes conflicts with the need to protect its users from abusive interactions. Balancing this ecosystem requires innovative solutions, which have included improved reporting mechanisms and account suspension policies. But as technology evolves, so too do the tactics of those who seek to abuse it, keeping Twitter always a step behind the next threat.

Commercialization represents another significant hurdle. Twitter has revolutionized global communication, yet translating its widespread influence into financial success has been a continuous struggle. Unlike platforms reliant on private user data for highly targeted advertising, Twitter's value proposition has always centered around its public conversations. Convincing advertisers of the utility of this broad-reach model versus more data-specific information poses ongoing strategic challenges.

Leadership decisions have also shaped Twitter's evolutionary path. Management changes often come with shifts in vision and goals, influencing everything from user experience to company culture. For Twitter, maintaining a consistent identity while navigating these internal modifications has been key to its ongoing relevance in the social media sphere.

Despite these challenges, the potential for reinvention keeps Twitter relevant. Its exploration into new features, like longer tweets, live streaming, and Twitter Spaces, illustrates a willingness to adapt while attempting to remain true to its core. This adaptability is vital for survival in a social media industry that is as competitive as it is volatile.

Still, Twitter's story offers numerous lessons for entrepreneurs and tech enthusiasts alike. It highlights the importance of innovation that responds to real-world needs, along with the balancing act between openness and control. Navigating these dynamics requires an understanding of not just user desires but also the broader social implications of any technological platform.

Ultimately, Twitter continues to grapple with its role as both megaphone and moderator. For it to thrive, addressing these challenges head-on with thoughtful strategies will be necessary. This involves careful consideration of content policies, user experience innovations, and financial models that ensure sustainability while supporting the vibrant, dynamic conversations that define its space. It's a testament to the power of vision and perseverance in the tech industry—principles that echo throughout this social media revolution.

Chapter 6: E-Commerce Giants

In the vast and ever-evolving landscape of e-commerce, few titans stand as tall and formidable as Amazon and Alibaba. Their stories are lessons in audacity and strategic brilliance, each carving out a unique yet overlapping sphere of influence that extends across continents and markets. Amazon's ascent wasn't just about books and CDs; it embodied a relentless quest for innovation, transforming retail through logistics mastery and an uncanny understanding of consumer behavior. Meanwhile, Alibaba redefined global reach by harnessing the collective power of small businesses and leveraging China's booming market, all while navigating complex regulatory landscapes. Together, they illustrate a powerful narrative of how digital platforms can transcend geographical and cultural boundaries, reshaping global commerce and setting new benchmarks for what's possible in a connected world. Their journeys inspire entrepreneurs to think bigger, act bolder, and reimagine the boundaries of trade in the digital age.

Amazon's Market Conquest

In the vast landscape of e-commerce, few stories capture the imagination quite like Amazon's remarkable rise. Emerging from the tech crucible of the mid-1990s, Amazon started as an unassuming online bookstore. Today, it stands as a titan of retail, a symbol of relentless ambition, and the kind of innovation that defines a generation. The narrative of Amazon's market conquest is one of strategic foresight, adaptability, and an unyielding focus on customer satisfaction.

Amazon's journey began in 1994 when Jeff Bezos spotted an opportunity at the intersection of the internet and retail. Amid the dot-com frenzy, Bezos understood that the internet could revolutionize how people shop. With a vision that extended far beyond books, he created a platform that would eventually cater to nearly every imaginable consumer need. The initial plan was simple yet groundbreaking: offer customers a variety of books in a digital format that physical stores couldn't match.

This strategy was bolstered by early adopters of the online shopping model, but it was Bezos's keen insights and customer-centric focus that set Amazon apart. He championed a company culture that prioritized the customer above all else. From the very beginning, customer reviews, personalized recommendations, and a seamless user interface became pivotal aspects of Amazon's website. This commitment to the user experience wasn't just theoretical; it was put into practice with initiatives like Amazon Prime, a game-changer that not only enhanced customer loyalty but also locked in a recurring revenue stream.

Prime was more than a loyalty program; it was a genius move that defined Amazon's approach to market expansion. Customers paid a flat annual fee for two-day shipping on a myriad of products, effectively making the vast selection of the e-commerce site as immediate as a trip to a local store. Over time, Prime evolved to include a host of other benefits, such as streaming services that rivaled the likes of Netflix, and exclusive deals that kept members deeply integrated into Amazon's ecosystem. Such inclusivity wasn't about profit margins alone; it was about making Amazon indispensable in everyday life.

Part of what drove Amazon's success was its relentless pursuit of growth and innovation. New ventures like Amazon Web Services (AWS) expanded the company's footprint beyond retail, tapping into the burgeoning world of cloud computing. By providing scalable computing power to businesses and individuals, AWS not only supplemented Amazon's income but also fortified its positioning in the tech industry. This diversification was a masterstroke that insulated the company from retail market volatility and kept its innovation flywheel in perpetual motion.

Amazon also displayed an uncanny ability to enter and redefine established markets, transforming them with its digital-first approach. The Kindle, for example, revolutionized how people consumed written content. By offering an entire library in a lightweight device, Amazon underscored its commitment to making content more accessible and ensuring it remained at the forefront of media distribution. This wasn't just about capturing market share from traditional booksellers but about creating a whole new way of reading and consuming content.

Moreover, Amazon's strategic acquisitions played a significant role in enhancing its market dominance. The purchase of Whole Foods in 2017 was a bold move that signified a serious play in the grocery sector, blurring the lines between online and offline retail. Through Whole Foods, Amazon gained not only a physical presence but also access to a demographic loyal to organic and fresh produce. It served as a testing ground for innovations like cashier-less stores, further cementing Amazon's role as a pioneer of retail technology.

What truly sets Amazon apart, though, is its willingness to invest in the future—often in areas that seem far removed from its core business. Take, for example, the ambitious projects under Amazon's Advanced Technologies initiative, ranging from delivery drones to AI-driven customer service. This transformative vision isn't about immediate returns but about planting seeds that could disrupt industries in years to come.

Yet, Amazon's reach hasn't come without scrutiny. Its sheer size and influence have raised questions about monopoly and antitrust practices. Critics argue that its dominance stifles competition and innovation in the retail space, forcing smaller players either to innovate or to risk obsolescence. These concerns are compounded by discussions around worker rights and the ethical implications of automation. The debate over Amazon's place in the economic landscape is ongoing, reflecting broader questions about the balance between innovation and equity.

Despite these challenges, Amazon's journey offers a masterclass in the art of business pivoting and scaling. It's a textbook example of how a company can leverage its strengths, yet adapt to changing market dynamics in pursuit of overarching goals. Entrepreneurs and business students can glean valuable insights from Amazon's trajectory: staying nimble, relentlessly prioritizing the customer, and thinking decades ahead rather than being mired in the present.

In the final analysis, Amazon's market conquest is a tale of visionary leadership combined with strategic execution. Its ability to continually reinvent itself while maintaining core values illustrates the power of a clear mission coupled with the courage to tread into uncharted territories. For those who aspire to follow in its footsteps, the lesson is that the journey of building an e-commerce giant is not just about riding the waves of technological change but about anticipating them and being prepared to ride the next wave, no matter how distant it may seem.

Alibaba and Global Reach

Alibaba's journey is one of incredible ambition and strategic foresight that has redefined e-commerce on a global scale. Founded in 1999 by Jack Ma, Alibaba's story is one of audacity, vision, and adaptability. At its core, the mission was simple yet far-reaching: to make it easy to do business anywhere. This seemingly straightforward goal was the vehicle through which Jack Ma sought to connect small businesses in China with international buyers and suppliers, fostering a comprehensive digital marketplace.

From its humble beginnings as a B2B marketplace connecting Chinese manufacturers with overseas buyers, Alibaba quickly expanded its reach. Jack Ma's recognition of the potential for a massive online consumer market in China led to the launch of Taobao in 2003, a C2C platform that soon dwarfed eBay's presence in the Chinese market. What set Taobao apart was its understanding of local consumer culture, offering free listings to incentivize sellers and incorporating a social element that resonated with users. This approach not only attracted buyers and sellers en masse but also disrupted the e-commerce landscape by prioritizing community engagement over mere transactions.

The introduction of Alipay in 2004 marked another pivotal moment in Alibaba's expansion, highlighting the importance of trust and security in online transactions. This digital payment platform provided an escrow service that alleviated the apprehensions surrounding online shopping. By solving a critical bottleneck, Alibaba was able to further accelerate its growth. Moreover, Alipay's success laid the groundwork for what would eventually become the Ant Group, showcasing Alibaba's knack for identifying and capturing synergistic opportunities.

Strategic alliances played a crucial role in Alibaba's global journey. Recognizing the importance of partnerships in extending its reach, Alibaba entered into various collaborations. Its 2014 initial public offering (IPO) on the New York Stock Exchange was a milestone, raising a record $25 billion. This not only underscored the market's confidence in Alibaba's prospects but also symbolized its transition from a national leader to a global powerhouse.

Alibaba's global strategy involved leveraging its technological innovations to cater to diverse markets. The acquisition of stakes in companies like Lazada in Southeast Asia and Paytm in India showcased its intent to tap into emerging markets with untapped potential. In these regions, Alibaba applied its expertise in logistics and digital payments to overcome local challenges, adapting its business model to fit different economic and cultural landscapes. Its Cloud Computing division, Alibaba Cloud, further cemented its global footprint, offering robust services that rivaled even established Western counterparts.

Crucially, Alibaba's understanding of the interplay between technology, culture, and consumer behavior propelled its success. By prioritizing customer experience and harnessing data analytics, Alibaba refined its services to meet users' evolving expectations. Initiatives like Singles' Day, which has become the world's largest online shopping festival, exemplify Alibaba's innovative approach to retail. This annual event generates record-breaking sales and reflects Alibaba's uncanny ability to blend commerce with entertainment, creating a consumer phenomenon recognized worldwide.

Alibaba's influence extends beyond commerce into logistics, entertainment, and even financial services, forming a multifaceted ecosystem that continues to disrupt traditional industries. With Cainiao, its logistics affiliate, Alibaba redefined supply chain efficiency, enabling faster delivery at scale across its network. In the entertainment sector, through its flourishing digital media and entertainment arm, Alibaba Pictures, it's carving a niche by merging content creation with e-commerce platforms, offering unique content-driven purchase pathways.

Despite its achievements, Alibaba faces challenges. Regulatory scrutiny and geopolitical tensions present significant hurdles, as seen in its recent confrontations with Chinese regulators. These challenges demand agility and adeptness in navigating complex legal and operational landscapes. In response, the company has diversified its investments across sectors perceived as future-proof, reaffirming its adaptability and commitment to sustained innovation.

The future for Alibaba involves not just fending off rivals but also identifying avenues for new growth, like artificial intelligence, new retail concepts, and the expansion of cloud services. As Alibaba endeavours to shape the future of global commerce, it aims to enrich its cultural perceptions and understanding of international markets, paving the way for a more interconnected and experiential digital marketplace.

Ultimately, Alibaba's story is a testament to the transformative power of vision and strategy. Entrepreneurs and business leaders can learn from Alibaba's ability to anticipate market shifts and integrate technology in ways that effectively meet consumer demands. Jack Ma's leadership philosophy emphasizes resilience and a deep commitment to core values, suggesting that success in the bustling e-commerce world involves more than just market connections—it's about creating opportunities, building trust, and nurturing a culture of relentless innovation.

Chapter 7: The Mobile Era

The Mobile Era ushered in a seismic shift in how businesses, and indeed the world, operated. As smartphones became ubiquitous, they transformed from mere communication devices into powerful mini-computers, capable of running complex apps that fueled a new wave of innovation. The titans of tech, embroiled in the so-called Smartphone Wars, competed fiercely to capture the imaginations and loyalty of consumers worldwide. Opportunities abounded for entrepreneurs willing to tap into the burgeoning app ecosystem, resulting in unprecedented market dynamics. This era redefined connectivity, leveling the playing field for startups to develop mobile solutions that could reach millions globally, often outpacing well-established companies in agility and innovation. The Mobile Era didn't just change the way we interact with technology; it also redefined strategic approaches within the tech industry, offering profound lessons for ambitious entrepreneurs looking to ride the next wave of technological evolution.

The Smartphone Wars

As we delve further into the mobile era, we find ourselves in the midst of the "Smartphone Wars," a period that redefined how individuals communicate, work, and interact with the world around them. It was a time when innovation wasn't just encouraged; it was essential. The stakes were high, and the players involved were some of the most formidable in the tech industry. Companies weren't just competing for market share; they were vying for influence over how societies functioned. The pressure to innovate fueled an environment of relentless creativity and bold gambles.

The launch of Apple's iPhone in 2007 was the catalyst that shifted the landscape in unimaginable ways. When Steve Jobs introduced the iPhone, it wasn't just a phone; it was a culmination of a vision for a smart, connected future. Touchscreens, app stores, and the idea of having the world at your fingertips were new terrains that competitors were quick to explore and exploit. This wasn't just about technology—it was about reshaping the economic and cultural fabric of everyday life.

Nokia, once a titan in the mobile phone industry, suddenly found its dominance threatened by the advent of this new paradigm. The Finnish company, which had pioneered mobile communication, struggled to adapt. They possessed the legacy and the expertise in mobile phones, but the ground shifted rapidly beneath their feet. This is a stark reminder that in the tech world, resting on laurels can be perilous. It's not just about having the best technology today but anticipating the needs of tomorrow.

Meanwhile, Google's Android platform emerged as a formidable competitor to Apple's iOS. Initially launched in 2008, Android's open-source nature was a game-changer. It allowed hardware manufacturers like Samsung, HTC, and LG to adopt the software and tailor products catering to various market segments—from budget phones to premium flagship devices. This democratization of the smartphone software landscape sowed the seeds for Android's eventual dominance in global market share.

The strategic decisions made by companies during the smartphone wars emphasized the importance of ecosystem building. Apple championed a closed ecosystem that integrated hardware, software, and services seamlessly. The App Store became a significant revenue stream and a powerful draw for developers and consumers alike. Google, on the other hand, leveraged its strength in data and search capabilities to develop a software-centric approach that fed into its other services, like Maps and Google Photos.

One can't ignore Samsung's role in this battle. As a hardware giant, they quickly adopted Android and became one of its most prominent benefactors, innovating relentlessly to close the gap with Apple. Their Galaxy series became a household name and highlighted how hardware innovation could coexist with the existing software ecosystem. The rivalry between Apple and Samsung became legendary, marked by patent wars and marketing jabs that captivated global audiences.

Amidst the titans, smaller companies found niches where they could excel. BlackBerry, once a leader in mobile phones thanks to its qwerty keyboards and secure messaging, faced existential challenges. While BlackBerry's decline highlighted the perils of not evolving with market shifts, it also underscored that innovation often requires a willingness to let go of past success and venture into uncharted territories.

There was also the compelling story of Microsoft's Windows Phone. Despite significant resources and expertise, Microsoft struggled to gain traction. Their experience stressed the critical lesson that timing and adaptability are crucial. Being innovative isn't solely about cutting-edge technology; it's about understanding and anticipating consumer needs and market dynamics.

As the dust began to settle, new players eyed the battles from different angles. Companies such as Huawei and Xiaomi from China started to make significant strides, capitalizing on the growing smartphone demands in emerging markets. They combined aggressive pricing strategies with solid hardware, positioning themselves as disruptive forces in the global market.

The smartphone wars left an indelible impact on how tech companies strategize and evolve. It highlighted the convergence of technology and lifestyle, where devices are not just tools but extensions of personal identity and capability. For business entrepreneurs and startups, this era serves as a powerful case study in adaptability, market insight, and the balance between competition and collaboration.

Entrepreneurs were inspired to rethink traditional business models, taking cues from how smartphone pioneers leveraged cross-industry synergies. Decades-old notions of product life cycles were overturned as software updates began to extend hardware utility beyond initial sales. The focus shifted from one-time purchases to ongoing consumer relationships, emphasizing an iterative, customer-focused approach.

Moreover, the era nourished the app ecosystem, creating untold opportunities for developers, designers, and dreamers worldwide. It gave rise to multitudes of new startups and business models that harnessed the power of mobile connectivity, altering how we order food, hail a ride, or even manage our finances.

The lessons from the smartphone wars resonate across industries. They teach us about the relentless pursuit of improvement, the courage to disrupt oneself, and the value of understanding shifting landscapes. Just as important is recognizing the importance of timing, the power of ecosystems, and the potential behind strategic alliances and open collaboration.

As we look to the future, the echoes of these battles will continue reverberating through generations, offering insights and inspiration for aspiring entrepreneurs and seasoned veterans alike. The smartphone wars were not merely a competition among corporations; they were a turning point that highlighted human creativity, ambition, and the relentless drive to connect the world.

App Ecosystem and Opportunities

The dawn of the mobile era wasn't just about sleek devices that fit into our palms; it marked the beginning of a vast ecosystem where apps became the lifeblood driving unprecedented opportunities. Apps have reshaped industries, altered consumer behaviors, and provided fertile ground for a new breed of entrepreneurs. Their development and proliferation signal a dynamic shift, creating a platform for innovation that's accessible, scalable, and bursting with potential.

At the heart of this evolution is the accessibility of app development. Unlike traditional software development, creating an app today doesn't require vast resources or a team of specialists. With platforms like Apple's App Store and Google Play, individual developers and small teams can reach millions worldwide. This democratization has fueled a surge of creativity, allowing anyone with a good idea to potentially disrupt existing industries. A lone programmer in a garage can now challenge established giants, forever altering the playing field.

The opportunities within the app ecosystem extend beyond individual success stories. Entire industries have been born within the confines of mobile apps. Consider the gig economy: companies like Uber and Airbnb rewrote the rules of transportation and hospitality using robust app-based platforms. These transformations unveiled new avenues for revenue and challenged traditional business models, forcing industries to adapt or risk obsolescence.

Mobile apps have also enabled a deeper understanding of consumer behavior. The data generated by user interactions provides insights that are invaluable to businesses. This data can precisely tailor marketing strategies and product offerings, aligning them with consumer preferences. Such personalization was once the domain of luxury brands; now, it's accessible to any enterprise with an effective app strategy.

Moreover, the app ecosystem thrives on collaboration and integration, leading to synergies that enhance user experience and functionality. Apps are increasingly avoiding insularity, opting instead for interconnectivity with other apps and services. Consider how apps integrate with social media platforms, payments systems, and even other apps to provide a seamless, holistic experience. This trend doesn't just improve usability but also opens up strategic partnerships, enhancing value for end-users and developers alike.

While opportunities abound, the app ecosystem also presents challenges that budding entrepreneurs must navigate. The sheer volume of apps means competition is fierce. Standing out in a crowded marketplace requires more than just an innovative idea; it demands flawless execution, astute marketing, and a deep understanding of user needs. It's a landscape where mediocrity is rewarded with obscurity, and only excellence attracts attention.

As the app ecosystem matures, it is also evolving toward inclusivity and accessibility. Apps are now being designed with global audiences in mind from inception, considering languages, cultural preferences, and socioeconomic factors. This approach not only broadens market reach but also enriches the app's utility for users worldwide. The concept of "glocalization" has taken root, emphasizing the importance of crafting globally resonant experiences that feel locally relevant.

Entrepreneurs looking to dive into the app ecosystem must also grapple with the sustainability of their business models. Many apps monetize through advertisements, in-app purchases, or a combination of models; however, these revenue streams need to be balanced carefully to avoid alienating users. Subscription models have gained traction recently, offering a steady revenue stream while incentivizing developers to continually improve their offerings.

The advent of technologies like AR, VR, and AI within the app ecosystem is another frontier of opportunity. These technologies promise to redefine user interaction, offering immersive experiences that blend the digital and physical worlds. Entrepreneurs poised to capitalize on these emerging trends have the potential to lead transformative changes across sectors, from education to healthcare, retail to entertainment.

Furthermore, the potential for innovative collaborations between apps and hardware continues to grow. Devices now boast features like advanced sensors, augmented reality capabilities, and IoT integration that apps can leverage to enhance functionality and engagement exponentially. This symbiosis promises new horizons for creativity and utility, inviting entrepreneurs to think beyond the traditional app experience.

Navigating the app ecosystem also means engaging with ethical considerations and privacy concerns. With great data comes great responsibility, and today's users are more aware and protective of their digital footprints. Balancing the benefits of data-driven insights with the need for transparency and ethical stewardship is crucial for building trust and loyalty.

Ultimately, the app ecosystem is a vivid illustration of how technology can democratize entrepreneurship. It's a realm where innovation is bound only by the limits of imagination, presenting a canvas laden with possibilities for those bold enough to explore it. Entrepreneurs who embrace this dynamic environment can discover paths to success that are as varied and unique as the apps within this ecosystem.

Chapter 8: Cloud Computing

As we transition into the era of cloud computing, we're witnessing a shift that's reshaping not just our technological landscape, but the very foundations of modern business. With its roots in the pioneering efforts of Amazon Web Services, cloud computing is now a cornerstone of agility and scalability for enterprises worldwide. This paradigm allows startups and established companies alike to transcend traditional infrastructure limitations, tapping into vast computational resources on demand. As competitors enter the space, market dynamics evolve rapidly, fostering an ecosystem ripe for innovation and disruption. The cloud has not only democratized access to powerful technologies but also spurred a reinvention of business models, where success isn't measured by ownership but by access and adaptability. For entrepreneurs navigating this terrain, embracing the cloud's potential isn't just a strategic choice— it's a necessity in building resilient, forward-thinking enterprises prepared for the challenges and opportunities of tomorrow.

Amazon Web Services' Impact

In the vast and ever-evolving landscape of digital technology, Amazon Web Services (AWS) stands as a colossus that reshaped the business of computing. Long before AWS became a household name, businesses faced significant barriers to getting their ventures off the ground. High upfront costs for servers, networking equipment, and technical expertise were just some of the hurdles new companies needed to overcome. Then came AWS, which changed the game by providing on-demand cloud computing resources that made starting and scaling a tech venture infinitely more accessible and affordable.

AWS's inception was hardly serendipitous. Amazon, known primarily as an e-commerce giant, saw the potential to leverage its extensive infrastructure beyond retail. In 2006, Jeff Bezos announced AWS as a new model of IT infrastructure that could be rented like a utility, similar to electricity. This bold move turned Amazon from a digital marketplace into a cornerstone of the internet. Businesses no longer needed vast capital just for hardware. Instead, they could pay as they go, scaling resources according to need, which aligned beautifully with the unpredictable nature of startup growth.

This pay-as-you-go model sparked a revolution. AWS offered flexibility, reducing the friction that many startups experienced. The service empowered entrepreneurs to focus more on innovation and less on infrastructure, which fundamentally altered the startup ecosystem. Imagine being able to transform an idea into a globally available service within days. This new reality inspired a wave of creativity in tech, with companies able to deploy applications faster and focus more resources on the user experience rather than backend logistics.

Not only did AWS democratize access to computing power, but it also drove innovation by offering a suite of tools that continued to expand. The portfolio grew from simple storage and computing power to include databases, machine learning, analytics, and even quantum computing services. Each additional capability allowed companies to explore new business models without significant investments in proprietary technologies. This accessibility to sophisticated technological tools meant that not only entrepreneurs but also large corporations could experiment with data-driven decision-making and digital transformations.

The breadth of applications enabled by AWS is impressive. Companies like Netflix and Airbnb harnessed AWS's power to manage their global operations efficiently. Netflix, for instance, leveraged AWS for seamless content delivery to millions of its subscribers, using AWS's scalability to handle variances in viewer demand. Airbnb, on the other hand, relied on AWS to ensure a smooth, uninterrupted booking experience for millions of users worldwide, even as it scaled its operations across continents.

AWS's impact isn't confined solely to the technological realm; it has economic implications as well. By offering its IT infrastructure as a service, AWS lowers the barrier to entry for countless startups. Entrepreneurship has diversified because ideas aren't stymied by the lack of capital. More players mean increased competition and innovation. For Amazon, AWS has grown into a key revenue driver, contributing significant profits that dwarf those from its retail operations.

The profound effect of AWS on business operations extends to corporate culture and internal processes. With AWS simplifying the logistics of IT, companies turned their focus inward toward fostering creativity and strategic growth. By eliminating the complexities of managing physical infrastructure, businesses could allocate resources more efficiently, dedicating them to talent acquisition, market research, and product development.

As pivotal as AWS has been in shaping modern computing, it didn't emerge without competition. The seismic shift it initiated roused giants like Microsoft and Google, prompting them to develop their cloud services, Azure and Google Cloud Platform, respectively. This competition has propelled the technological advancements seen in cloud computing, leading to better services at lower costs, further benefiting the startup ecosystem.

Yet AWS's influence on the technology landscape transcends its immediate business gains. It embodies the spirit of Silicon Valley—a hotbed of ideas, risk-taking, and constant disruption. AWS teaches us a critical lesson about the nature of innovation: often, the most transformative advancements spring not from the core competency of an organization but from an unforeseen need or opportunity. Jeff Bezos did not set out to build one of the world's most used cloud platforms when he founded Amazon, yet by recognizing a need and taking an audacious leap, AWS was born.

In conclusion, AWS has fundamentally altered how we think about computing. By removing traditional barriers to IT resources, it has democratized access to technology, given rise to countless successful startups, and prompted innovations in business strategies across industries. This remarkable transformation isn't just a story of technological advancement; it's an inspiration—a testament to how one company's venture into the unknown can foster unprecedented change and empower countless others to dream bigger and achieve more.

Competitors and Market Shifts

The cloud computing landscape is a dynamic tableau, constantly shifting as new competitors enter the arena and established players vie for dominance. In the early days, Amazon Web Services (AWS) paved the way, transforming a nascent idea into a thriving multi-billion-dollar industry. This transformation didn't happen in isolation, though. It spurred action and reaction, with other tech giants taking notice and realigning their strategies to enter this lucrative space.

Microsoft and Google have been formidable AWS competitors, each bringing its strategic advantages to the table. Microsoft's Azure leverages its enterprise expertise, seamlessly integrating with widely-used products like Office and Windows Server. It's a natural fit for businesses that were already entrenched in the Microsoft ecosystem and needed an intuitive transition to the cloud. Microsoft's strength lies in its ability to offer hybrid solutions that blend on-premises and cloud computing, meeting the varied needs of enterprise clients.

Google Cloud Platform (GCP) distinguishes itself by capitalizing on Google's prowess in data analytics and machine learning. With roots deep in search and AI, GCP offers sophisticated tools for data scientists and developers looking to tap into Google's famous algorithms and infrastructure. Their strategies revolve around appealing to startups and tech-savvy enterprises ready to embrace the next wave of data-centric computing. GCP's support for global-scale data processing and innovation-driven culture has attracted businesses looking to leverage powerful AI capabilities.

Behind these well-known giants, smaller and more niche players like IBM, Oracle, and Alibaba Cloud bring unique flavors to the cloud computing menu. IBM focuses on blockchain technology, AI, and enterprise-grade solutions, primarily appealing to its long-standing customer base in industries like finance and healthcare. They've positioned IBM Cloud as a leader in industry-specific cloud solutions, with a clear focus on security and compliance.

Meanwhile, Oracle, with its stronghold in database technologies, offers a robust cloud service fine-tuned for managing complex data workloads typical of large corporations. Oracle aims to cement its position by enabling more seamless transitions for its existing customers moving to cloud infrastructure. Alibaba Cloud, although initially catering mainly to the Chinese market, has expanded its horizons by targeting countries across Asia and beyond, creating fierce competition for global players hoping to penetrate these emerging markets.

As competition intensifies, shifts in market dynamics are often catalyzed by technological breakthroughs and shifts in consumer demand. Companies constantly enhance their services—introducing multi-cloud strategies, serverless computing, and edge computing to meet the ever-evolving needs of their customers. There's a notable increase in hybrid cloud models offering businesses the flexibility to enjoy both public and private cloud benefits while optimizing cost and efficiency.

The advent of 5G technology, with its promise of ultra-fast connectivity and low latency, adds an additional layer of complexity and opportunity. Cloud services are increasingly pivotal as they facilitate the seamless deployment of applications that will rely on 5G speed, from augmented reality to real-time data analytics. Companies are harnessing this potential, ensuring their infrastructures can support the expansive data flow that 5G will introduce.

Market shifts are further fueled by increasing attention on data sovereignty and privacy regulations. As different countries implement stringent data protection laws, cloud providers are compelled to build local data centers to comply, affecting their global strategies significantly. These legal frameworks shape the competitive playing field by dictating how and where data can be processed and stored, impacting operational costs and service delivery approaches.

Sustainability also emerges as a critical factor in shaping cloud computing's future. Businesses are increasingly conscious of their carbon footprint, pushing providers to integrate green technologies into their offerings. Providers invest in renewable energy and energy-efficient data centers, capitalizing on sustainability as a competitive advantage. AWS,

Google, and Microsoft have made significant public commitments to reduce their environmental impact, recognizing that sustainability can drive customer loyalty and innovation.

In this rapidly evolving context, the ability to adapt swiftly and innovate continuously isn't just beneficial—it's required. Cloud providers dedicate substantial resources to research and development, ensuring that they stay at the forefront of technological advancement. Those who succeed will be companies that anticipate market shifts and pivot swiftly to align their strategies with emerging trends and technologies.

The narrative of cloud computing doesn't merely reflect competition among tech giants; it signifies profound shifts in how businesses operate and how individuals consume technology. For entrepreneurs and business students, understanding these dynamics is crucial. It goes beyond mere awareness—it's about leveraging insights to innovate and maneuver effectively in a highly competitive environment. As the clouds race forward, driven by the winds of technological change, they create a vista of unpredictable opportunities and challenges, inviting the boldest to carve out their markets.

Chapter 9: The Gig Economy

The Gig Economy has redefined traditional labor paradigms, ushering in a seismic shift in how we understand work in the digital age. Spearheaded by trailblazers like Uber and Airbnb, this movement has catalyzed an era where flexibility trumps stability and innovation upends convention. For entrepreneurs, it's a landscape bursting with opportunities and challenges, a testament to how technology can catalyze economic and social transformation. Unlike the rigid structures of yesteryear, this economy favors the nimble—those who can swiftly pivot and adapt to evolving market needs. But it's not just about providing convenience or earning a quick buck. It's about weaving an intricate tapestry that interlinks technology, autonomy, and customer-centric models, creating value in ways previously unimagined. The narrative of the Gig Economy is motivational; it underscores the relentless drive and creative zeal vital for startup success. Entrepreneurs who dare to engage with its complexities will find not only disruption but also a wealth of potential, ripe for those willing to grasp it with both hands.

Uber's Industry Shakeup

In the grand tapestry of modern business, few companies have altered the contours of an industry as much as Uber. It's not just the idea of a convenient ride at your fingertips that Uber harnessed; it's the entire framework of what work could look like in the 21st century. Uber epitomizes a new rhythm in employment, resonating with the flexibility yet unpredictability that defines the gig economy. The tale of Uber isn't merely about a ride-sharing app; it's about shaking the very foundations of industry norms.

Uber's rise to prominence wasn't just about the technology, though the smartphone app was certainly revolutionary. It was the company's ability to identify and exploit inefficiencies in the existing transportation services that set it apart. Traditional taxi services were bogged down by regulation and supply constraints. Uber saw an opportunity to leapfrog these barriers through an innovative approach, creating a marketplace where demand instantly met supply—anyone with a car and some free time could serve as a driver.

It was a disruptive model that both seduced and scared its competitors. The ability for customers to track their rides, predict costs upfront, and pay effortlessly via app signaled a tectonic shift. This shift was not just in service delivery but also in customer expectations. Uber leveraged technology to redefine convenience, creating an unprecedented level of service that quickly turned into an expected norm. Was it magic? Not quite. It was the very epitome of innovative thinking, where Uber didn't just challenge the status quo—it reinvented it.

Beyond the customer experience, Uber's greatest shakeup came with its reimagining of the employer-employee dynamic. In the traditional employment model, jobs come with contracts, benefits, and expected hours. Uber challenged this paradigm, offering instead a flexible income stream that matched modern-day aspirations for many seeking part-time or supplementary work. However, this flexibility came with its own share of debates—debates about stability, benefits, and what constituted genuine employment.

The implications of Uber's model reach far beyond its own operations. The gig economy's rapid growth has catalyzed substantial regulatory and societal conversations. Cities around the world have grappled with how to classify Uber drivers—are they independent contractors or employees deserving of benefits? Each city and country faced this legal conundrum, resulting in a patchwork of policies that still cause friction in Uber's operations today.

Despite these challenges, Uber's model has undeniably inspired a host of startups and industries to rethink their approach. Delivery services, freelance platforms, and even professional services have been influenced by the gig economy's allure. Industries are reconfiguring, not just because of Uber's footprint but the broader acceptance that flexibility and instantaneous service are now key drivers of consumer satisfaction and employee engagement.

With all its innovations and disruptions, Uber also faced significant hurdles. Criticisms about driver wages, safety concerns, and corporate culture controversies have peppered its journey. Yet, these challenges also reflect the growing pains of trailblazers on an uncharted path. The fact that Uber continues to thrive speaks to its resilience and adaptability. In moments of crisis and scrutiny, the company has pivoted, adjusting its strategies to align more closely with regulatory and societal expectations.

However, it's not just about overcoming challenges. There's also a lesson to be learned in how Uber scaled its operations globally. It navigated diverse markets, each with its own regulatory and consumer behavior patterns, showcasing an understanding of when to adapt and when to hold firm. Leveraging local knowledge, Uber was not just exporting a model; it was engaging in a global dialogue about ride-sharing and its potentials.

Uber's impact isn't limited to business and economics. It's also a cultural phenomenon. The term "Uber" has become a verb—a linguistic marker of its influence. The very act of altering language illustrates its deep integration into our daily vocabulary and lives. Through its name, Uber encapsulates not only a service but an era—a testament to how rapidly digital innovations can embed themselves into the social fabric.

As we reflect on Uber's industry shakeup, the lessons are many. The company's journey provides valuable insights for entrepreneurs and established businesses alike. It highlights the importance of challenging conventional wisdom, embracing technology, and understanding the evolving needs of the market. At its core, Uber turned the mundane into the extraordinary and, in doing so, it changed how we perceive transportation, work, and technology.

Ultimately, Uber's story is a narrative of innovation, resilience, and transformation. It serves as a compelling reminder that industries aren't static; they're pliable, ready to be reshaped by those who dare to think differently. For those inspired by the confluence of technology and entrepreneurship, Uber's journey offers a treasure trove of insights into how the future of business can be crafted—by challenging norms, harnessing technology, and adapting to the ever-changing winds of consumer expectation.

Airbnb's New Hospitality Model

The gig economy has fundamentally altered how people conceive of work and employment. Among the pivotal players in this transformation, Airbnb has redefined hospitality, blending elements of technology, trust, and community. This new model deviates sharply from traditional hospitality paradigms, pushing boundaries and reshaping consumer expectations. Entrepreneurs can learn much from how Airbnb leverages the assets of the gig economy while fostering a unique brand experience.

At the core of Airbnb's success is the simplification of home-sharing. It recognized a crucial gap in the market—many travelers sought unique accommodations that hotels couldn't provide, while property owners had underutilized spaces. By bridging this gap, Airbnb managed to create a platform that connects people with complementary needs, resulting in a win-win situation for hosts and guests. This innovative move democratizes hospitality, granting anyone with a spare room the opportunity to become a part-time hotelier.

Airbnb's narrative isn't just about providing alternative accommodations —it's about crafting experiences. They've introduced the concept of "live like a local," offering travelers not just a place to stay, but an opportunity to immerse themselves in the culture of their chosen destination. For business students and tech enthusiasts, this goes beyond simple market exploitation; it's a masterclass in brand differentiation and value addition. The startup managed to create a narrative that resonates with customers itching for authentic experiences and willing to pay for the privilege.

One of the most striking facets of Airbnb's model is the element of trust it fosters between strangers. Traditionally, such trust would be mitigated by the presence of institutional regulations. Airbnb, however, employs user reviews, verification systems, and community guidelines to establish and maintain trust. This peer review system builds a community ethos and is an exemplary model of how digital platforms can encourage positive and self-regulating interactions. It's not just about technology but human psychology, an understanding of which is crucial for entrepreneurs looking to create peer-to-peer platforms.

Airbnb also illustrates the power of leveraging existing resources without the need for heavy capital investment. Unlike traditional hotel chains requiring significant capital expenditure for construction and maintenance, Airbnb's model allows for scalability with comparatively minimal investment. This feature is especially interesting for budding entrepreneurs who might think substantial capital is necessary to compete in industries traditionally dominated by infrastructural behemoths.

Another key point of Airbnb's success lies in its data-driven approach. The company deftly utilizes data analytics to optimize user experience, personalize recommendations, and improve operational efficiency. Data helps Airbnb to track market trends, analyze customer feedback, and develop strategies to tweak their offerings. For contemporary entrepreneurs, this illustrates the indispensable role of data in strategy formulation and execution, emphasizing the need to incorporate robust analytics from early stages of business development.

Airbnb's focus on community was further enriched by the development of Airbnb Experiences, a platform that allows local hosts to offer activities ranging from cooking classes to city tours. This diversification expands Airbnb's offerings beyond accommodations into a more holistic travel service. Strategically, it extends the brand into new revenue streams while deepening customer engagement. This move demonstrates how startups can sustain growth by continually exploring ancillary products and services that align with their core values.

Of course, the journey hasn't been without challenges. Regulatory hurdles, community pushback regarding local housing shortages, and the impact of the COVID-19 pandemic have all tested Airbnb's resilience. However, its ability to pivot and adapt speaks to an essential entrepreneurial quality—agility. Airbnb's approach to adversity underscores the necessity for businesses to be nimble and responsive to both market conditions and regulatory landscapes.

What about ethical considerations? Airbnb's model raises questions regarding its impact on local communities and housing markets. By incentivizing short-term rentals, critics argue it may exacerbate housing shortages in some areas. Here lies a crucial learning opportunity: the importance of balancing growth with social responsibility. Entrepreneurs must weigh the consequences of disruptive business models on broader societal scales, ensuring that their innovations do not inadvertently cause harm.

The influence of Airbnb on the gig economy further illustrates how startups can transform traditional industries. Inspired entrepreneurs should take to heart the company's ability to craft a unique and scalable service model, leverage technology, and foster community trust. Such insights are invaluable in navigating the complex landscape of startups and embody the agile, innovative spirit necessary for success in today's competitive environment.

Thus, Airbnb's hospitality model serves as a beacon of what's possible when entrepreneurs dare to challenge the status quo. The company's trajectory highlights the significance of identifying market voids, leveraging existing assets, and staying adaptable amidst uncertainties. For those aspiring to effect similar transformative changes, the Airbnb story offers a compelling roadmap.

Chapter 10: The Role of Venture Capital

In the ever-evolving landscape of technology and startups, venture capital (VC) plays a pivotal role. It acts as the financial lifeblood that fuels innovation and propels fledgling companies toward growth and success. VCs don't just provide money; they're catalysts for change, offering strategic guidance and connections that can turn a brilliant idea into a market-successful enterprise. At its core, venture capital is about risk and reward—investors are willing to take on considerable risk for the potential of substantial returns, often betting on unproven technologies and audacious visions. The influence of VCs extends beyond monetary investment; it's about nurturing visionaries who dare to challenge the status quo and reshape industries. As we dive into the dynamics of funding stages and the ever-shifting trend patterns in VC investments, it's evident that understanding the role of venture capital is essential for anyone navigating the startup ecosystem. This unique symbiosis between entrepreneurs and capitalists isn't just about dollars and cents—it's about making possibilities endless.

Funding Stages and Functions

The journey of a startup from conception to a booming business is akin to a hero's journey, teeming with challenges, triumphs, and the critical guide known as venture capital. Understanding the stages of funding and the function each one serves is vital for any entrepreneur striving to convert their vision into a sustainable reality. This roadmap not only illuminates the path from seed to series and beyond, but also highlights the strategic roles venture capital firms play in nurturing nascent companies.

At the genesis of a startup's life, the seed stage emerges. Picture a lone inventor in a garage or a small team huddled around a dining table, armed with nothing but a brilliant idea and boundless enthusiasm. Here, seed funding, often sourced from angel investors, friends, family, or very early-stage venture capitalists, provides the vital resources needed to flesh out proof of concept. It's a time for creating minimum viable products, conducting initial market research, and setting the foundation for future growth.

This stage often demands a high tolerance for risk. Investors aren't just gambling on a product; they're betting on people. They seek passionate, resilient founders who can pivot and adapt as reality smacks up against the drawing board. Hence, the function of seed funding extends beyond financial sustenance to include mentorship, providing entrepreneurs with the insights needed to refine their strategies.

Once a startup has found its footing with a solid product-market fit, it progresses to the Series A stage. This is where the narrative starts to mature. The focus shifts from exploration to execution, and businesses need resources to scale their operations and fine-tune their revenue models. At this point, the founders' vision should start to materialize into tangible metrics—early customer traction, revenue consistency, and a clear growth strategy.

Series A funding generally involves more significant sums from institutional investors who are now interested in detailed business plans backed by robust data. The role of venture capitalists at this juncture isn't just about funding expansion, but also facilitating strategic partnerships, making key hires, and providing governance oversight as part of the board. They're essentially shaping the fledgling company into one of the dominant players in their market niche.

Following Series A, a startup may pursue Series B and C rounds, each representing further steps on the scaling ladder. In Series B, the business gears up for rapid growth, investing heavily in sales, marketing, and new product development. This is the stage where the startup must demonstrate that it can win in competitive landscapes, capturing significant market share and fending off emerging threats.

Series C and beyond typically indicate a company that's nearing maturity, preparing to either go public or be acquired. Here, the influx of capital is often used for acquisitions, new market expansion, or developing additional product lines, ensuring they maintain competitive advantage. In these later rounds, investors may include not just venture capital firms but also private equity firms, banks, and hedge funds, each bringing a blend of resources and networks to the table.

While these stages paint a linear path, the journey is anything but straight. Many startups experience circuitous routes, perhaps requiring bridge funding or facing down-rounds when targets aren't met. This landscape is rife with complexity, but it also offers diverse opportunities for growth and learning. Success hinges not just on securing funds, but on utilizing them strategically and effectively.

Yet, no discussion on venture capital's role would be complete without acknowledging the subtle, often unstated, influences VCs have on company culture and ethos. The relationship between investor and founder is symbiotic—a delicate balance of guidance and autonomy. Venture capitalists bring more than cash to the table; they bring vision, experience, and access to networks that can catapult a startup from obscurity to the spotlight.

Moreover, they act as catalysts, igniting innovation through their emphasis on scalability and sustainability. This is where the motivational aspect of venture capital truly shines. Founders are pushed to dream bigger, to tackle larger markets or even global issues, all while maintaining the agility and creativity that sparked their journey.

One might say venture capital transforms dreams into enterprises, enabling the seemingly impossible. As much as entrepreneurs crystallize ideas into products, venture capitalists articulate those products into markets. Their role, in essence, is not merely to finance but to elevate and propel human ingenuity to its fullest potential.

As you contemplate the road ahead, whether as an entrepreneur or an investor, remember that understanding these funding stages and functions is like harnessing a powerful toolset. It's about making informed choices, timing your moves, and collaborating with the right partners at each turn. Like the auditoriums filled with the sharp minds of Silicon Valley, or the buzzing cafes of startup hubs worldwide, the world of venture capital is alive with possibilities.

It's no wonder that embracing this funding journey with strategic foresight and adaptability is pivotal to lasting success in the tech industry. With ample preparation and an open mind, each challenge becomes an opportunity to innovate, iterate, and ultimately, to inspire. This narrative, filled with a blend of ambition and pragmatism, aligns perfectly with the great entrepreneurial stories of our time, ready to carve new paths in the landscape of business.

Notable VCs and Investment Trends

Understanding the intricacies of notable venture capitalists (VCs) and investment trends provides a window into the ever-evolving world of startups and innovation. Venture capital, the lifeblood of entrepreneurial ventures, has transformed the business landscape countless times by backing daring ideas that have turned into industry standards. To grasp the monumental role VCs play, it's essential to recognize not only the key players but also the strategic trends shaping this domain.

One of the most noteworthy figures in venture capital is Sequoia Capital. Founded in 1972 by Don Valentine, Sequoia has been instrumental in funding landmark companies like Apple, Google, and WhatsApp. With a keen eye for potential, Sequoia Capital's influence has resonated throughout the technology sector, providing the critical support that enabled these businesses to flourish. Their approach, often described as hands-on, reflects a desire not just to offer financial backing but also strategic oversight.

Beyond individual firms, investment trends reveal much about the underlying movements in the startup ecosystem. Among these trends, the rise of unicorns—startups valued at over $1 billion—has captured much attention. This trend hints at a significant willingness among investors to back high-risk ventures on the promise of exponential returns. Silicon Valley, being the nucleus of tech innovation, has been the breeding ground for these unicorns, but the phenomena are not confined to just one region.

Another profound trend is the surge in interest toward sustainable and socially responsible investing. With consumers increasingly favoring eco-friendly and ethical practices, VCs have redirected attention to ventures that align with these values. Funds specializing in clean technology and renewable energy projects have emerged, marking a shift that integrates societal benefits with business profitability.

Furthermore, geographical diversification has come into sharper focus. While Silicon Valley remains a formidable hub for tech startups, VCs are exploring opportunities globally. Cities like Berlin, Bangalore, and Shanghai have blossomed into significant tech ecosystems. This globalization of venture capital illustrates an eagerness to tap into diverse talent pools and untapped markets, amplifying the reach and impact of technological innovation worldwide.

Tech-savvy investors like Andreessen Horowitz are notable for pioneering this global perspective. Founded in 2009 by Marc Andreessen and Ben Horowitz, the firm champions investments across various continents and industries, often looking to capitalize on disruptive technologies. By aligning with groundbreaking ventures across disparate markets, Andreessen Horowitz exemplifies strategic investment, adaptive to the swell and ebb of technological trends.

In addition to geographic expansion, sectoral shifts play a pivotal role in defining investment landscapes. The recent focus on artificial intelligence, machine learning, and blockchain technology indicates a strong venture backing towards digital transformation. These domains promise sweeping changes across industries, and VCs have consistently sought to position themselves at the forefront of these technological advances.

The coalescence of AI and blockchain, for instance, illustrates a promising frontier. Startups leveraging these technologies are developing solutions that increase efficiency, security, and transparency across various sectors, from finance to logistics. As a result, funds directed towards these innovations have soared, fueling a rapidly progressing tech landscape.

Some VCs, like Kleiner Perkins, have made it their mission to identify the next big thing in these evolving sectors. Known for their backing of pioneers like Amazon and Twitter, Kleiner Perkins has continued to fund ventures that push the boundaries of what is technically feasible, demonstrating a commitment to sustaining the disruptive ethos that defines Silicon Valley.

Despite these advances, the venture capital landscape is not immune to shifts in economic conditions. Recessions and market downturns inevitably impact funding availability. In periods of economic contraction, VCs may become more conservative, prioritizing investments that promise a clearer path to profitability. Yet, history shows that some of the most successful startups have emerged in challenging economic times, underscoring the resilience and adaptability required in venture investing.

In recent years, there's been a marked focus on the democratization of venture funding. Emerging platforms that connect a broader swath of investors with burgeoning startups are gaining traction. By lowering traditional barriers to entry, these platforms empower more participants to engage in venture financing, thereby diluting the risk and increasing the pool of potential capital.

Finally, the Covid-19 pandemic undeniably catalyzed a shift in investment strategies. Remote work technologies, digital healthcare solutions, and e-commerce witnessed unprecedented investment inflow as demand for innovative digital solutions skyrocketed. This crisis-driven pivot emphasizes venture capital's role as a responsive change agent, unraveling new opportunities amid uncertainties.

In closing, notable VCs and investment trends offer a dynamic tableau that continually redefines the trajectory of technology and innovation. The ability of VCs to adapt and anticipate shifts in societal, technological, and economic landscapes is paramount. Their astute decisions fuel startup growth, fostering environments where groundbreaking ideas can thrive. As entrepreneurs, business students, and tech enthusiasts forge ahead, understanding these venture dynamics becomes key to navigating, and ultimately succeeding in, the competitive world of startups.

Chapter 11: Women in Tech

In the ever-evolving landscape of technology, women have been quietly yet powerfully reshaping the narrative. While the industry was once dominated by male figures, a growing number of women are breaking through barriers, leading successful startups, and driving innovation that challenges the status quo. This chapter sheds light on their journeys, painting a picture of resilience amid the ongoing gender equality challenges that persist in tech. Women have proven that their perspectives are not only valuable but crucial, inspiring an entire generation to defy stereotypes and pursue ambitions without hesitation. The fight for equal representation is far from over, yet every step forward signifies hope and change, pushing the boundaries of what's possible in this dynamic field. Through understanding and effort, the tech space can become a beacon of diversity and inclusion, setting an example for other industries to follow.

Breaking Barriers and Achieving Success

Women have been making remarkable strides in the tech industry, breaking glass ceilings and inspiring future generations. Yet, this journey has been neither straightforward nor easy. Women in tech have had to navigate a path riddled with challenges—ranging from enduring stereotypes to overcoming institutional hurdles. Their journey, however, is a powerful testament to resilience and ingenuity.

It's no secret that tech has historically been a male-dominated field. Icons like Ada Lovelace and Grace Hopper were among the exceptions, pioneering what we now know as computer programming and algorithm design. For decades, their contributions were undervalued, their narratives lost in the overarching history of technological development. The recent resurgence in recognizing their stories is not just acknowledgment but a reclamation of a space that women have always contributed to, albeit invisibly.

The rise of women in tech over the last few decades is largely attributed to a combination of factors, including the advocacy for STEM education among women, networking opportunities, mentorship programs, and the establishment of supportive communities. Organizations have sprouted, dedicated to providing resources and encouragement for women in tech, aiming to make boardrooms and innovation labs more inclusive spaces.

Women, when given the opportunity, have made transformative contributions to the tech industry. Consider Sheryl Sandberg's role in scaling Facebook to new heights or Susan Wojcicki's leadership at YouTube. These aren't just roles fulfilled but blueprints of success crafted against cultural and systemic odds. Each story is a mosaic tile in the larger picture of what women can achieve in an environment that supports and values their contributions.

However, breaking barriers doesn't happen in isolation. It requires ongoing effort, both from individuals and organizations. Corporate leadership must champion diversity not just in hiring practices but in creating an environment where all voices are heard and valued. Diverse teams are known for their robustness, bringing different perspectives that lead to innovative solutions. It's a win-win that companies invest in—expansive creativity and a balanced organizational ecosystem.

One such example can be seen in the strategic initiatives led by companies like Google and Microsoft. They have implemented wide-reaching programs designed to close the gender gap, not only elevating women to high-ranking positions but actively reshaping how tech organizations function. These efforts include flexible work policies, enhanced parental leave, and employee resource groups that foster dialogue and inclusion.

Meanwhile, many startup founders have taken personal journeys to turn barriers into stepping stones. Women in tech have become increasingly visible and vocal in entrepreneurial arenas, founding companies that reflect not only technological prowess but diverse and inclusive values. They continue to challenge the status quo, redefining traditional structures and promoting gender equality in their own way.

The importance of mentorship cannot be overstated. Mentorship can be a pivotal component in preparing the next generation of women leaders. Seasoned female tech professionals impart wisdom and guidance, their insights lighting the path for young women seeking to thrive in the industry. Mentorship programs also serve as a network of support, providing tools and strategies to tackle the challenges unique to women in tech.

Moreover, the rise of networking events specifically tailored for women in tech promotes community and helps cultivate long-lasting professional relationships. These gatherings are not just platforms for exchanging business cards; they're crucibles of innovation, where ideas flourish and partnerships take root. Women supporting women—whether through webinars, conferences, or hackathons—creates a nurturing ecosystem that reinforces solidarity and progress.

It's crucial to acknowledge that progress doesn't come without setbacks. Gender bias persists in many quarters, subtle yet insidious, affecting career progression and job satisfaction. Women are still underrepresented at the two ends of the career spectrum: entry-level positions and leadership roles. Addressing these disparities requires vigilance and a commitment to continuous improvement, both within organizations and the broader tech community.

The era of digital transformation presents a unique opportunity. As industries shift towards remote work and decentralized teams, there's an unprecedented potential for gender equality. Geographic barriers that once constrained career growth are dissolving, creating opportunities for a broader, more diverse talent pool to participate in the tech landscape.

Corporate responsibility plays a critical role here. It encompasses more than diversity quotas; it involves creating equitable spaces where women —and all underrepresented groups—can thrive. Embedding diversity in the company culture and operational processes transforms corporate responsibility into corporate advantage, resulting in better decision-making and star performance across all metrics.

As we move forward, the narrative around women in tech will continue to evolve. Institutional changes, individual success stories, and the ever-present push for gender equality create momentum. Entrepreneurs, policymakers, and tech leaders must consistently question how they can contribute to crafting a more equitable tech industry. The investment in diversity and inclusion today will pay dividends tomorrow—a maxim evidenced by the growing number of women leading groundbreaking ventures and initiatives.

In the end, the story of women in tech isn't just about breaking barriers. It's a chronicle of courage, perseverance, and innovation that defies the odds and reshapes the future of technology. It's a testament to what can be achieved when opportunity meets talent, where a collective commitment to equity becomes the catalyst for success.

Ongoing Gender Equality Challenges

In the realm of technology, where innovation knows no bounds, the persistent challenge of gender equality stands as a critical barrier to achieving true inclusivity. While strides have been made, and many glass ceilings shattered, ongoing challenges remain that call for concerted efforts from all corners of the industry. These hurdles are not just societal or cultural; they're intricately woven into the fabric of the technology ecosystem, impacting women across all levels of tech development, leadership, and participation.

For decades, computing has been predominantly male-centered, with women often occupying roles that lack visibility and decision-making power. Despite being pivotal in the nascent stages of computer programming, notably during the World War II era, women have seen their roles diminished, overshadowed by their male counterparts. This historical narrative, while slowly being rewritten, continues to echo in today's tech landscape, influencing hiring practices, workplace culture, and industry perceptions. The irony remains palpable—an industry characterized by its progressive breakthroughs, struggling with an age-old issue: gender disparity.

The statistics are telling. Women represent a minority in technical positions within companies renowned for their innovation. In many large tech firms, women hold less than a quarter of technical roles, and the number dwindles further when it comes to leadership positions. This disparity isn't a reflection of capability or ambition but rather a systemic issue that begins with education and permeates through hiring, promotion, and work culture. It's a cycle of underrepresentation, often starting in school with lower enrollment rates in STEM programs among female students due to stereotypes and lack of encouragement.

In examining the causes, unconscious bias surfaces as a critical factor. It's not always about intentional discrimination but rather ingrained perceptions and stereotypes that subtly influence decision-making processes. These biases manifest in various facets of the workplace—

from the hiring and evaluation processes to the allocation of tasks and opportunities for advancement. Women, more often than not, are the victims of these biases, facing an uphill battle to prove their worth in spaces that are unduly skeptical of their capabilities.

Another formidable challenge is work-life balance, which disproportionately affects women. The tech industry's demanding hours and often inflexible environments make it difficult for those with caregiving responsibilities, who are primarily women, to climb the career ladder. Despite the advent of remote work—which offers some flexibility—the expectation to be perpetually available persists, seeping into personal time and space. Hence, creating environments that genuinely support balanced lifestyles is imperative if the industry is to retain diverse talent.

Tackling these challenges requires a multipronged approach. It begins with education and mentoring. Educational institutions play a pivotal role in shaping the future workforce by encouraging young women to pursue STEM fields and providing role models who can inspire. Mentorship programs within organizations help bridge the gap between entry-level roles and executive positions, offering support and guidance to navigate the professional landscape.

Policies promoting gender diversity must be more than performative gestures. Companies ought to establish goals for hiring and promoting women, closely tracking progress and holding leadership accountable. Transparency in salary reports and promotion statistics can aid this process, fostering an environment that discourages bias and encourages equity. Moreover, promoting diverse leadership not only helps reveal biases but also showcases different leadership styles and skills that can benefit the organization as a whole.

However, policy changes alone cannot transform culture. Building an inclusive workplace demands commitment at all organizational levels, led by example from the top. Creating safe spaces for dialogue and incorporating feedback mechanisms can enhance understanding and catalyze meaningful change. Ensuring a culture of acceptance and belonging can unleash creativity and innovation, as diverse teams bring varied perspectives and problem-solving approaches.

Moreover, systemic challenges call for a redefinition of success in tech. Emphasizing collaboration over competition, valuing diverse contributions, and adopting a holistic approach to talent evaluation can mitigate some of the adverse effects of traditional gender roles. Women in technology should not only aim for parity in numbers but equitable treatment in recognition, opportunity, and compensation.

Yet, one cannot overlook the role of allies in this journey. Men, holding the majority of leadership positions, have the power and responsibility to advocate for gender equality actively. By challenging stereotypes, calling out biases, and supporting their female counterparts, they can be instrumental in driving change. The path towards equality is not one women should tread alone; it requires solidarity from all communities within the tech industry.

As the narrative continues to evolve, it's essential for budding entrepreneurs and future leaders to adopt these lessons early on. By fostering a culture that values diversity from the outset, startups and new enterprises have the unique opportunity to redefine industry standards and blaze a trail towards an equitable future. The transformation won't happen overnight, but consistent, conscious efforts could bring about a paradigm shift.

The ongoing challenges to gender equality in tech are a reminder of the work still needed. They're more than just obstacles—these challenges are opportunities for growth, innovation, and progress. They call for a collective resolve to create an industry that not only thrives on cutting-edge advancements but also truly reflects the diversity and inclusivity it hopes to inspire. It's a journey worth undertaking, one where the future isn't just imagined—it's collectively shaped by every talented individual given a fair chance to contribute.

Chapter 12: Cybersecurity and Privacy Concerns

As the digital landscape evolves, entrepreneurs and tech enthusiasts can't ignore the mounting cybersecurity and privacy issues that threaten innovation. These concerns have grown alongside the tech industry's rapid expansion, drawing attention from governments, businesses, and consumers alike. Data breaches have not only cost companies fortunes but have also eroded consumer trust, emphasizing the need for robust protective measures. In response, regulatory frameworks have emerged, attempting to keep pace with technological advancements while empowering companies to innovate securely. It's crucial for startups to integrate security measures into their business models from the outset, balancing technological progress with the protection of sensitive data. Motivation lies in transforming these challenges into opportunities, pioneering solutions that safeguard privacy while driving forward the tech frontier. With the interconnectedness of today's world, understanding and addressing cybersecurity and privacy concerns isn't just a box to check—it's a competitive edge that leaders can leverage to inspire confidence and collaboration in the digital age.

Data Breaches and Consequences

In the digital age, where information is more valuable than ever, data breaches have become a menacing reality. The tech ecosystem, continuously advancing at a breakneck pace, faces an omnipresent threat: the unauthorized exposure of sensitive information. As businesses increasingly rely on technology and cloud-based solutions, they also become more vulnerable to cyber threats. For entrepreneurs and business enthusiasts, understanding this landscape is crucial not just for mitigating risks but also for harnessing opportunities in cybersecurity innovations.

Data breaches aren't just about stolen information; they unveil myriad consequences that can unravel the fabric of any organization. When a breach occurs, the most immediate impact is often financial. The costs associated with responding to a breach can be astronomical. Companies are forced to invest in damage control, which includes legal fees, compensation to affected customers, and heightened security measures. Moreover, there are hidden costs such as loss of customer trust and potential revenue decline. A breach can tarnish a brand's reputation overnight, leading to long-term financial repercussions that could cripple a business.

The equifax breach of 2017 serves as a stark reminder of the dire consequences data breaches can entail. It exposed the personal information of over 140 million people, culminating in a significant loss of consumer trust and settlements amounting to hundreds of millions of dollars. This incident underscores the criticality of robust cybersecurity measures, not just as a defense mechanism but as an integral part of business operations. Entrepreneurs must view cybersecurity expenditure as an investment rather than a cost.

It's not only large corporations that need to be wary. Startups and smaller businesses are equally at risk, often more so due to limited resources and less sophisticated security infrastructure. A survey reveals that nearly half of small businesses suffer cyberattacks, yet many underestimate the likelihood. For startups possessing valuable intellectual property or customer data, an attack can be debilitating and might even shorten the company's lifespan before it truly begins.

Beyond financial and reputational damage, there are legal implications and regulatory pressures following a breach. Governments worldwide have started imposing strict data protection laws—such as the EU's General Data Protection Regulation (gdpr) and the california consumer privacy act (ccpa)—to hold companies accountable for the data they handle. Non-compliance can lead to hefty fines, making it imperative for businesses to understand and implement these regulations thoroughly.

While regulatory frameworks aim to protect consumer data and privacy, they also present an opportunity. Entrepreneurs can innovate by creating compliance solutions and cybersecurity services that address these requirements. As a growing field, cybersecurity offers immense potential for startups willing to dive into this niche and address the gaps in the current security infrastructure.

The psychological impact on consumers should not be underestimated. When individuals feel their personal data isn't secure, it impacts their willingness to engage with businesses online. The relationship between a company and its customers is built on trust, and once broken, it is challenging to mend. Businesses must prioritize transparent communication during breaches, assuring customers that corrective actions are being taken.

We must also consider the internal ramifications within organizations. Following a breach, employee morale can drop as trust in the organization's capability to protect its data wavers. Employees may feel their efforts have been undermined, leading to decreased productivity. Leaders in tech must ensure that cybersecurity becomes a shared responsibility within their teams, promoting a culture of vigilance and continuous learning in security measures.

However, like many challenges faced by businesses, data breaches also catalyze growth and innovation. When businesses encounter the aftermath of a breach, it often pushes them to re-evaluate and bolster their security practices. This necessity for improvement drives the market for newer, more adaptive cybersecurity technologies. Entrepreneurs are presented with the challenge of creating products and services that can outpace hackers and offer robust protection to consumers.

As technological landscapes evolve, so do the tactics of cybercriminals. An unfortunate but essential reality is that every new innovation potentially leads to new vulnerabilities. Thus, the quest for cybersecurity is ongoing, demanding agility, vigilance, and adaptation. Entrepreneurs venturing into the digital frontier must recognize both the threats and the opportunities that data breaches present.

It's a complex dance—balancing security against innovation, risk against reward. Entrepreneurs in the tech industry must rise to the occasion by embedding robust cybersecurity measures from inception rather than retrofitting them post-breach. In doing so, they not only protect their creations but also set industry standards that safeguard the broader digital future.

Regulatory Responses and Innovations

As we've progressed further into the digital era, the intersection of technology and regulation has emerged as a dynamic frontier. Entrepreneurs, business students, and tech enthusiasts see this as an area ripe for opportunities and pitfalls alike. The rapid acceleration of technological advancements, paired with increasing cybersecurity threats and privacy concerns, has necessitated a robust and adaptive regulatory environment. But regulation isn't just a set of constraints; it's also a catalyst for innovation.

The cybersecurity landscape is ever-evolving. Every new piece of technology introduces potential vulnerabilities. This inevitability fuels a cat-and-mouse game between cybersecurity experts and cybercriminals. Amidst this backdrop, regulatory bodies across the globe have been forced to evolve swiftly. Their mission: to protect data integrity and consumer privacy while not stifling technological progress. It's a balancing act, one that requires ingenuity and foresight.

In the early days, regulatory measures were often reactive rather than proactive. They aimed at damage control after high-profile breaches. However, the current regulatory responses have shifted to a more preventive approach. Initiatives like the General Data Protection Regulation (GDPR) set the stage by encouraging companies to take privacy by design and data protection seriously. Such regulations showcase how proactive measures can influence the ethos of tech companies, nudging them toward more ethical data management practices.

Innovation in this context isn't merely about creating new technologies but also about finding new ways to secure them. As cybersecurity threats became more sophisticated, so too did the technological responses. Advancements such as artificial intelligence and machine learning are now at the forefront of developing robust cybersecurity measures, capable of anticipating and mitigating threats in real time. Entrepreneurs entering this space are not only innovating but also contributing to a safer digital environment for all.

Moreover, there's an exciting interplay between regulation and entrepreneurship. While regulations might seem restrictive at first glance, they can spur entrepreneurs to break new ground by developing compliant technologies that also outperform competitors. This phenomenon is evident in the rise of regtech—regulatory technology—a sector dedicated to helping businesses comply with regulations more efficiently. Offering solutions like automated compliance checks and real-time monitoring, regtech has become a burgeoning market ripe with possibilities for startups.

This wave of regulatory innovations doesn't stop at compliance tools; it extends into the realm of new business models and strategies. Digital certifications and privacy-centric services are emerging, allowing companies to build trust with consumers by transparently showcasing their adherence to privacy norms. This trust-centric model is fast becoming a differentiator in a crowded market, giving compliant businesses a competitive edge.

Startups venturing into privacy-enhancing technologies (PETs) are also making waves. These innovations revolve around user privacy and anonymization techniques, which ensure that data does not identify individuals while still allowing for meaningful analytics. By championing these approaches, startups can align their missions with the growing consumer demand for privacy and ethical data usage, turning regulatory pressure into a business advantage.

The interplay between cybersecurity regulations and innovations also has macroeconomic ramifications. Silicon Valley, once the unchallenged epicenter of tech innovation, now shares the spotlight with global hubs partly due to varying regulatory landscapes. Countries with supportive regulatory frameworks have seen a surge in tech startups, indicating that the path to innovation isn't just about technology but also about crafting environments where technology can thrive securely and ethically.

Collaborative initiatives between governments and tech industries represent another exciting frontier. By bringing tech innovators to the regulatory table, we tap into a wellspring of creativity while ensuring that regulations consider real-world applications. This partnership model can drive policies that are both pragmatic and forward-thinking, benefiting tech industries while safeguarding consumer interests.

For entrepreneurs, understanding the framework of regulations is as crucial as understanding market dynamics. They must navigate this intricate landscape with an eye towards compliance without losing sight of their innovative potential. In doing so, they can transform regulatory challenges into business opportunities.

In conclusion, regulatory responses to cybersecurity and privacy concerns are not just about curbing threats. They're about steering the tech industry towards a future where innovation goes hand in hand with responsibility. For those ready to embrace the challenges posed by these regulations, there's a world of opportunity to redefine what it means to be at the cutting edge of technology, proving that regulations, when embraced rather than resisted, can be catalysts, not constraints. The key to success lies in this nuanced dance between compliance and creativity, and in harnessing the power of regulation as a springboard for innovation.

Chapter 13: Artificial Intelligence Advancements

In an era where the boundaries of technology are constantly pushed, artificial intelligence stands at the frontier, transforming the way businesses operate and innovate. Entrepreneurs see AI not only as a tool for enhancing efficiency but also as a catalyst for entirely new business models. Its applications are diverse, from automating mundane tasks to generating insights from massive datasets, enabling companies to make data-driven decisions like never before. However, with transformative power comes ethical considerations—balancing innovation with responsibility remains a complex challenge. As AI technologies continue to evolve, they proffer endless possibilities, compelling tech innovators to ponder the broader impacts on society, the workforce, and privacy. Navigating this landscape requires a delicate balance of ambition and ethics, promising both risks and unprecedented opportunities for those willing to chart this new territory.

Transformative Technologies and Applications

With the relentless advancement of artificial intelligence, we're witnessing a seismic shift in the technological landscape. Transformative technologies are not just changing industries; they're redefining the paradigms of innovation and growth. Entrepreneurs and tech enthusiasts alike must pay close attention to these developments as they hold the keys to unlocking unprecedented opportunities.

Consider, for instance, the integration of AI in healthcare. Autonomous systems capable of diagnosing diseases, predicting patient outcomes, and even suggesting treatment plans are no longer a distant dream. AI-powered diagnostic tools have already begun to surpass human doctors in terms of accuracy for certain conditions. This transformation not only promises higher accuracy and efficiency but also has the potential to make healthcare more accessible to underserved populations. The ripple effect extends to startups and innovators, who now have the chance to create solutions that were once unimaginable.

In the realm of finance, AI's applications are equally groundbreaking. Algorithms now perform tasks like risk assessment and fraud detection with precision and speed that humans simply can't match. By analyzing vast datasets, AI-driven fintech solutions are enabling personalized banking experiences, automating trading and investment strategies, and streamlining regulatory compliance. For entrepreneurs ready to capitalize on these trends, the barriers to entry in finance tech have lowered, opening a plethora of avenues for innovation and disruption.

Moreover, AI is revolutionizing the world of marketing as well. Predictive analytics and customer insights, driven by machine learning algorithms, allow companies to tailor experiences like never before. From personalized advertising campaigns to dynamic pricing models, AI empowers marketers to craft strategies with higher ROI. Startups leveraging these capabilities can level the playing field with larger competitors, harnessing the power of data to win customer loyalty and drive growth.

Another fascinating application of AI lies within the transportation industry. Self-driving vehicles, once confined to the pages of science fiction, are inching closer to reality thanks to machine vision and deep learning algorithms. These transformative technologies promise to reshape urban landscapes, reduce traffic fatalities, and improve accessibility. For entrepreneurs, the autonomous vehicle sector offers a fertile ground for developing new business models, particularly in logistics, ride-sharing, and urban planning.

AI has also made significant strides in education, where adaptive learning platforms are transforming traditional classrooms. By customizing curricula to fit individual student needs, AI can enhance learning outcomes and democratize access to quality education. Startups in the edtech space stand at the forefront of this transformation, with opportunities to innovate in content delivery, assessment methods, and lifelong learning solutions.

Even the creative industry is not immune to AI's transformative potential. Tools powered by AI are generating art, music, and writing, offering unprecedented assistance to human creativity. These applications can inspire entrepreneurs to explore synergies between AI and human artistry, ultimately leading to unique products that captivate audiences worldwide. The convergence of creativity and technology is a fascinating frontier, ripe for those daring enough to venture into it.

Looking at the manufacturing sector, AI applications are advancing the concept of smart factories. Automation, coupled with real-time data analysis, is driving efficiencies at unprecedented levels. Predictive maintenance, supply chain optimization, and quality control are just some areas where AI acts as a catalyst. For startups, the opportunity here is to provide solutions that bridge gaps in this ecosystem, offering tools and technologies that enhance the manufacturing process.

Energy management is another domain that's being fundamentally altered by AI technologies. Smart grids and energy consumption forecasting are optimizing resource distribution and minimizing waste. Entrepreneurs who innovate in this space may not only capitalize on the growing demand for sustainable solutions but also contribute significantly to combating global climate challenges.

Lastly, consider the impact of AI in retail. From inventory management to personalized shopping experiences, AI is streamlining operations and facilitating customer-centric strategies that drive sales and improve satisfaction. Retail startups can use AI tools to build scalable and responsive business models that adapt to consumer preferences quickly and efficiently.

AI's journey is a vivid example of how transformative technologies are shaping the modern world. For entrepreneurs and business leaders, the key to leveraging these advancements lies not just in recognizing potential applications, but in understanding the broader implications of these technologies. The future belongs to those who can merge innovation with execution, tapping into AI's capabilities to create products, services, and experiences that resonate in an increasingly tech-driven society.

These transformative technologies not only open new horizons but also herald the emergence of new ethical, cultural, and social discussions. As AI continues to evolve, it becomes essential for entrepreneurs to engage in conversations about its impacts, ensuring that technological advancements align with societal values. Only then can we harness AI's potential to build a future that's both innovative and equitable.

In the end, the ability to foresee and adapt to these technologies marks the difference between thriving in the digital age and becoming obsolete. In an ever-accelerating world, those willing to embrace change and understand its implications are best positioned to lead and inspire the next wave of entrepreneurial success.

Ethical Considerations and Risks

Artificial intelligence (AI) is transforming industries at an unprecedented rate, bringing with it complex ethical considerations and risks that entrepreneurs and business leaders must confront. As AI technologies continue to evolve, they're not just reshaping business landscapes but are also challenging existing ethical norms and raising new questions about responsibility, fairness, and transparency. In this chapter, we'll explore some of the most pressing ethical issues and risks associated with AI advancements.

The power of AI lies in its ability to process vast amounts of data and generate insights that can drive decision-making. However, this capability also raises significant privacy concerns. As AI systems collect and analyze personal data, they often operate with minimal oversight, potentially leading to breaches of individual privacy and exploitation of sensitive information. Many businesses are now grappling with how to balance leveraging AI for competitive advantage while respecting users' privacy rights.

Bias is another critical ethical dilemma in AI development. AI systems are only as unbiased as the data they are trained on. If these data sets reflect human prejudices or systemic inequalities, AI can perpetuate and even amplify these biases. This becomes problematic in areas like hiring, where biased algorithms can unfairly disadvantage job applicants based on race, gender, or other characteristics. As companies increasingly deploy AI in areas that impact people's lives, ensuring that these technologies are fair and unbiased becomes paramount.

Transparency in AI decision-making processes is another ethical challenge. Often, AI operates in a "black box," where the rationale behind its decisions isn't clear, even to its creators. This opaqueness can lead to mistrust and resistance from users and customers who want to understand how decisions affecting them are made. Striking a balance between competitive secrecy and necessary transparency is an ongoing struggle for AI-driven businesses.

Beyond individual businesses, AI poses broader societal risks. The automation of jobs through AI and machine learning technologies raises significant concerns about employment and economic stability. While AI can lead to innovation and efficiency, it also threatens to displace significant portions of the workforce. Entrepreneurs and leaders must consider how to retrain and reskill workers to thrive in an AI-driven economy, ensuring that technological progress benefits all members of society.

Another emerging risk of AI is its potential to be misused. Automated systems can be employed for malicious purposes, such as deepfakes or misinformation campaigns that can undermine democratic processes or harm individuals' reputations. Business leaders must be proactive in preventing the misuse of their AI tools and technologies, implementing safeguards to protect against these risks.

Responsibility in AI development goes beyond technical feasibility. Ethical AI requires thoughtful consideration of who gets included in its design and deployment process. Diverse teams are crucial for identifying potential biases and ethical concerns early in the development lifecycle. Entrepreneurs must foster an inclusive environment that encourages diverse perspectives to inform AI strategies.

Regulatory frameworks are gradually emerging to address these ethical and safety concerns. Governments and international organizations are beginning to formulate policies that outline ethical guidelines for AI development and deployment. Businesses need to stay informed about these regulatory trends to ensure compliance and to align their AI strategies with evolving legal standards. By proactively engaging with policymakers, businesses can help shape fair and effective regulations that encourage innovation while protecting societal interests.

As AI continues to integrate into decision-making processes, the question of accountability comes into sharp focus. When AI fails or causes harm, determining who is liable becomes complex. Is it the developer, the deployer, or the AI system itself? Clearly defined accountability structures are essential to ensure responsible AI use and to build trust with stakeholders.

Entrepreneurs and business leaders play a critical role in shaping the ethical landscape of AI. They must actively engage with ethical issues throughout the lifecycle of AI projects, identifying potential risks and implementing strategies to mitigate them. This involves choosing ethical partners, conducting impact assessments, and fostering a culture of continuous ethical reflection.

To navigate these ethical considerations successfully, businesses must look at them not just as compliance issues but as opportunities to differentiate themselves. Companies that prioritize ethical AI can build stronger brands, earn customer loyalty, and create sustainable business models that respect human rights and values. These ethical commitments can inspire innovation, unlocking new ways to solve societal problems through technology.

Ultimately, the ethical considerations and risks of artificial intelligence are as dynamic and diverse as the technology itself. As AI continues to advance, society, businesses, and individuals must remain vigilant about ethical boundaries and strive to align technological progress with human welfare. The story of AI isn't just about machines and algorithms—it's a narrative about our collective responsibility to craft a future where technology serves the greater good.

Chapter 14: The Promise and Peril of Crypto

In the whirlwind world of high-tech innovation, few phenomena have captured the imagination and sparked debate like cryptocurrency and blockchain technology. At the heart of this digital disruption, Bitcoin emerged as the flagship, its meteoric rise a compelling testament to both the allure and volatility of decentralization. Entrepreneurs and business visionaries are drawn to the promise held by these technologies: the potential to revolutionize financial systems, enhance transparency, and foster a new era of global connectivity. Yet, the accompanying perils are just as noteworthy, marked by market instability and intense regulatory scrutiny. The crypto space is a double-edged sword, where audacious ideas clash with real-world challenges, creating both opportunities and obstacles for startups and established enterprises. It beckons a deeper reflection on risk-taking, innovation, and the ever-evolving landscape of technological entrepreneurship.

Bitcoin and Blockchain Innovations

Bitcoin and blockchain have shaken the foundations of the financial world, offering a glimpse of how technology could redefine economies and societies. It's a narrative that's as compelling as any; it takes the audacity of entrepreneurs, the curiosity of technologists, and even attracts a fair share of skepticism from economists. However, the central tenet remains: cryptocurrency and blockchain technology propose a new way of thinking about trust, decentralization, and how we transact.

The birth of Bitcoin in 2009 was a clarion call for innovation in financial systems. Created by the mysterious Satoshi Nakamoto, Bitcoin proposed a simple yet transformative idea – a decentralized digital currency, free from institutional control. This was more than just a tool for payment; it was an open-source network, with its code available for examination and extension. The underlying technology, blockchain, became the hero – an unsettling, disruptive force for industries entrenched in traditional methods of ledger-keeping and transaction assurance. This decentralized ledger challenged the status quo by offering a way to eliminate middlemen, reduce transaction costs, and increase transparency.

Entrepreneurs quickly gravitated towards Bitcoin's potential to democratize finance. It wasn't just about currency anymore; it was about building a new digital economy. Blockchain offered fertile ground for innovation, encouraging developers to create decentralized applications that stretch beyond financial services. Smart contracts became a popular application, executing transactions once predefined conditions were met, without need for intermediaries. This opened doors for entrepreneurs to streamline processes in industries ranging from insurance to real estate.

Of course, the journey hasn't been without its hurdles. The scalability of Bitcoin remains a concern. As the network grows, so does the time and energy required to verify transactions. Yet, challenges are often precursors to innovation. Entrepreneurs and tech leaders are experimenting with solutions like the Lightning Network, aiming to speed up transaction times and lower fees for Bitcoin users. It's a vibrant, collaborative effort reflective of the startup culture of Silicon Valley, where rapid prototyping and agile development drive technological advancements.

Blockchain's wider-reaching impact is visible beyond Bitcoin. Cryptocurrencies have diversified, with Ethereum introducing a platform not just for currency but for decentralized apps. Ethereum's smart contracts and blockchain's programmability have ignited a revolution in Initial Coin Offerings (ICOs), decentralized finance (DeFi), and non-fungible tokens (NFTs). The implications for business are profound: new asset classes are emerging, investors are exploring alternative avenues for growth, and traditional institutions are being prompted to rethink their offerings.

Yet, with great promise comes significant peril. The regulatory landscape surrounding cryptocurrency is anything but settled. Entrepreneurs need to navigate a maze of legalities, with governments scrutinizing cryptocurrencies under their respective jurisdictions. Concerns about security, tax evasion, and the use of crypto for illicit activities often dominate headlines. However, these challenges shouldn't stifle innovation; rather, they should serve as catalysts for creating robust, compliant business models that leverage the strengths of blockchain while adhering to legal norms.

The transparency offered by blockchain technology also forces businesses to rethink their operational strategies. Firms considering blockchain must adapt to its immutable and transparent nature. This requires a cultural shift towards accountability and openness, which, although daunting, could foster increased trust and loyalty among stakeholders and consumers. For entrepreneurs, embracing this culture can be a vital differentiator in an increasingly competitive market.

The motivations for embracing these innovations are manifold. There's the allure of tokenizing assets, democratizing ownership, and providing liquidity to otherwise illiquid markets. There's also the wider social impact; blockchain can bring financial services to billions of unbanked individuals worldwide, challenging the traditional banking sector and opening up new markets. Entrepreneurs have the opportunity to address significant social issues, turning profit motives into forces for good.

Looking ahead, the potential to integrate blockchain with other emerging technologies is tantalizing. Powerful synergies could arise from blockchain's intersection with AI and IoT. For instance, using blockchain to ensure the integrity and security of data collected by IoT devices while employing AI to interpret this data promises revolutions not only in tech, but across industries from healthcare to logistics.

Ultimately, the story of Bitcoin and blockchain is still unfolding. The entrepreneurs and visionaries who dare to venture into this nascent landscape will be those who question what is possible, redefine what is probable, and provide real-world applications that change how we think about money, trust, and transactions. These leaders are not only shaping the future of crypto but are also writing a compelling chapter in the larger narrative of technological advancement and entrepreneurship. The path includes uncertainties, but the possibilities for impact and transformation are immense.

Regulatory and Market Volatility

The world of cryptocurrency offers both dazzling potential and daunting challenges. At its heart lies the promise of decentralization, financial inclusion, and transformative technological innovation. Yet, stirring beneath the surface is a stormy brew of regulatory dilemmas and market unpredictability. Understanding these forces is crucial for entrepreneurs, business students, and tech enthusiasts who seek to harness the power of crypto while navigating its turbulent waters.

When Bitcoin first emerged, it was synonymous with the dream of a financial system free from intermediaries and institutional control. This dream quickly attracted a mix of avid supporters and skeptical regulators. Governments worldwide grappled with this new paradigm, trying to strike a balance between embracing innovation and safeguarding economic stability. Blockchain, once seen as Bitcoin's accessory technology, became a standalone force, promising to revolutionize everything from supply chains to public records. However, the regulatory landscape around cryptocurrencies remains murky at best.

Regulatory bodies across the globe have adopted varied approaches to crypto. In the United States, the Securities and Exchange Commission (SEC) has become a formidable gatekeeper, scrutinizing Initial Coin Offerings (ICOs) and token classifications. In contrast, countries like Malta have positioned themselves as crypto-friendly jurisdictions, crafting legislation that encourages crypto businesses to set up shop. This diversity in regulatory response highlights a central tension: the need for regulation to protect consumers and ensure financial stability versus the imperative to foster innovation and stay competitive on a global stage.

Volatility is another defining feature of the crypto market. Price swings that would be deemed catastrophic in traditional markets are commonplace here. Bitcoin, for instance, has seen its value skyrocket to astonishing heights, only to plummet rapidly, leaving investors reeling. Newcomers to this space often find themselves overwhelmed, unable to predict the next tidal wave of change. This level of unpredictability serves as both a lure for speculators dreaming of overnight wealth and a deterrent for business leaders who favor more predictable markets.

For startups, the crypto sphere presents unique risks and opportunities. On one hand, the fluidity and openness of blockchain technology allow for the creation of innovative business models that challenge the status quo. On the other hand, the absence of clear regulatory frameworks in many places can be a double-edged sword. Companies must be nimble, ready to pivot their strategies as regulations evolve and as market conditions shift.

Moreover, how one interprets the regulatory actions matters greatly. In some cases, government intervention can be a catalyst for market stability and confidence. By clarifying how cryptocurrencies fit within existing financial regulations, authorities can actually encourage institutional investment, which in turn smooths out market volatility. Conversely, overzealous regulation could stifle creativity and force businesses to seek friendlier jurisdictions, resulting in a fragmented market landscape.

Statistical analysis of the crypto market reveals patterns of behavior during different levels of regulatory scrutiny. During periods of increased regulatory oversight, markets tend to stabilize as uncertainty decreases. Conversely, in periods of regulatory ambiguity, the market often becomes a hotbed for speculation, increasing the likelihood of extreme volatility. Entrepreneurs need to be aware of these trends and strategize accordingly.

Yet, the real power in navigating regulatory and market volatility lies in understanding the underlying technologies and societal shifts. Blockchain is not just a ledger but a philosophy of transparency and decentralization. Its very nature challenges the traditional gatekeeping roles of banks and governments. Entrepreneurs who grasp this can better anticipate where regulatory friction might occur and where opportunities for breakthrough exist.

Just as companies in the dot-com era rewrote the rules of communication and commerce, today's crypto enterprises are charting new ways to engage with capital and communities. However, they must do so with an eye to history. Learning from past cycles of boom and bust in technological revolutions, crypto pioneers can prepare for a future that's as unpredictable as it is promising. Market volatility doesn't just expose risk; it highlights areas ripe for innovation and evolution.

The sector is, after all, highly dynamic and responsive to broader economic conditions. Crypto markets do not operate in isolation but are influenced by global trends, from economic downturns to geopolitical tensions. Factors like inflation rates, international trade policies, and societal acceptance play crucial roles in shaping the regulatory context. As such, both startups and established players must remain informed of external influences to craft resilient strategies.

Despite the complexities, the aspirational vision of crypto as a democratizing force persists. The ultimate goal is not to eradicate regulatory systems but to integrate them into an ecosystem that respects both individual empowerment and collective security. Entrepreneurs equipped with this dual focus can navigate the volatility not just as a challenge but as a landscape ripe for transformative growth and enduring success.

Chapter 15: The Rise of Electric Vehicles

Just as combustion engines powered the 20th century, electric vehicles (EVs) are defining 21st-century transportation. Spearheaded by companies like Tesla, the EV revolution is more than just an industry shift; it's a reinvention of mobility, dramatically accelerating the move towards sustainability. As global consciousness leans towards environmental stewardship, entrepreneurs and startups have seized the opportunity, diving into electric vehicle development with unbridled innovation. This surge has catalyzed advancements in autonomy and infrastructure, overcoming hurdles of range anxiety with sprawling networks of charging stations. Such infrastructure is crucial in addressing consumer concerns and making electric vehicles a viable option for the masses. The industry's landscape is fiercely competitive, not just because of technological leaps, but also due to the passion of those who dare to disrupt. Visionary leaders, fueled by a mix of idealism and pragmatism, are at the forefront of this transformation, setting a high bar for traditional car manufacturers. In the coming years, as battery technologies advance and economies of scale drive costs down, the electrification of vehicles will likely become indispensable. Entrepreneurs who embrace this change will be positioned not just to ride the wave but to help shape the future of mobility. Thus, the rise of electric vehicles is not merely a narrative about cleaner energy; it's a testament to how innovation-driven by necessity can redefine industry paradigms and inspire a new generation of business pioneers.

Tesla's Disruption and Competition

Tesla's emergence marked a seismic shift in the automotive industry, historically dominated by internal combustion engines. Founded in 2003, Tesla's disruptive force isn't solely due to its electric vehicles (EVs), but also its bold mission to transition the world to sustainable energy. By reimagining the very notion of what a car could be, Tesla challenged both the technological status quo and the legacy strategies of established automakers.

Tesla's innovation journey began when the company launched the Roadster in 2008. At a time when EVs were often dismissed as impractical or too expensive, the Roadster proved that electric cars could be fast, efficient, and enjoyable to drive. This was more than just launching a product. It sent a message to the world: Electric didn't have to mean compromise. While critics initially viewed Tesla's ambitions with skepticism, the Roadster's success laid the foundation for Tesla's future models.

The real disruption came with the introduction of the Model S in 2012. This luxury sedan combined cutting-edge technology with exceptional performance, achieving accolades from both consumers and automotive critics. Its impressive range, innovative design, and robust performance shattered the previous perceptions of electric cars. In challenging the norm, Tesla didn't just transform its own business; it nudged the entire industry toward an inevitable electric future.

Tesla's relentless focus on accelerating the production of EVs has ignited a race in the auto sector that extends beyond electric propulsion. The company's direct-to-consumer sales model, over-the-air software updates, and Autopilot feature have reshaped industry expectations of customer experience and vehicle software. Such approaches have forced traditional automakers to reevaluate and adapt their own business models, lest they be left behind.

But Tesla's journey hasn't been without hurdles. Production challenges, market skepticism, and financial constraints have all threatened to derail its momentum. Yet, in each instance, Tesla has recalibrated and pushed forward. This resilience has often been fueled by Elon Musk's charismatic vision and unyielding determination to innovate. Through ups and downs, the company has become an emblem of how passion and perseverance can drive revolutionary change.

The competitive landscape in the electric vehicle market has also evolved dramatically. Once Tesla proved there was a market for high-performance electric vehicles, legacy automakers and newcomers alike began vying for a piece of the pie. Companies like General Motors, Ford, and Volkswagen invested billions into their respective electric vehicle programs, racing to catch up. Meanwhile, new entrants such as Rivian and Lucid Motors are looking to carve out their own niches in a burgeoning industry.

Though competition is fierce, Tesla maintains a strategic advantage with its early-mover status, integrated ecosystem of energy products, and a robust network of Superchargers. Its brand exudes innovation, alluring not just environmentally-conscious consumers but tech enthusiasts and pioneers. However, with great power comes great responsibility, and Tesla's dominance means that any misstep is closely scrutinized by investors and competitors alike.

The race toward autonomy is another competitive frontier where Tesla aims to keep its lead. The company's self-driving technology, though still in development, promises to change the way society thinks about transportation. If successful, Tesla's work in autonomy could redefine mobility, altering not just how we drive but potentially eliminating the need for drivers altogether.

As the electric vehicle space continues to grow, Tesla's challenge will be to maintain its innovative edge while scaling operations to meet global demand. This balance between innovation and scalability is crucial for sustaining leadership in the rapidly changing automotive industry. It's a delicate dance that requires agility and foresight, attributes Tesla has frequently demonstrated.

Looking ahead, Tesla's journey provides many valuable lessons for entrepreneurs and industry leaders alike. It's a testament to the power of visionary thinking, tenacity, and the readiness to embrace risk. Tesla's story encourages us to ask what might be possible when we look beyond the immediate and the traditional, daring to tread uncharted paths.

In the end, Tesla's disruption in the world of electric vehicles goes beyond cars. It's about transforming our approach to energy, sustainability, and technological innovation. As the chapters of the automotive industry continue to be rewritten, Tesla's narrative remains a compelling chronicle of unyielding ambition and transformative impact.

Evolution of Autonomy and Infrastructure

The landscape of electric vehicles (EVs) is undergoing a transformation, and at the heart of this change lies the evolution of autonomy and infrastructure. As EV technology advances, the integration of autonomous capabilities has opened new frontiers, while the corresponding infrastructure development is redefining collective mobility. These changes aren't happening in isolation; they're intricately connected, with each advancement in autonomy mirroring shifts in infrastructure development. This synergy is paving the way for a future where electric vehicles operate in a more seamless and efficient environment.

Autonomous driving technology has become a central focus of innovation within the automotive industry. The initial steps toward autonomy involved basic driver-assist features, like adaptive cruise control and lane-keeping assistance. Over time, these systems have evolved through machine learning and artificial intelligence, striving for full vehicle autonomy. Companies like Waymo, Tesla, and others are pouring resources into achieving what's often referred to as "Level 5" autonomy, where a vehicle can manage all driving tasks without human intervention under all conditions. The quest for this level of autonomy raises profound questions about safety, ethics, and the very nature of driving itself.

The advancements in autonomy have necessitated significant changes in vehicle infrastructure. Charging stations, once limited to urban centers and specific highway corridors, are now expanding to rural areas and high-density urban environments alike. Governments and private enterprises are collaborating in unprecedented ways to support this expansion. For example, initiatives to create smart charging networks, where vehicles can communicate with the grid to optimize charging times, are becoming a focus of infrastructure policy. This development not only makes EV ownership more convenient but is also crucial for integrating autonomous electric vehicles into daily life.

Innovation in infrastructure goes beyond just expanding charging networks. It's about creating a smart road ecosystem, which integrates vehicle-to-infrastructure communication. This means roads and cities could one day interact dynamically with autonomous vehicles to optimize traffic flow, reduce emissions, and enhance safety. For instance, traffic lights could adapt to the presence of autonomous EVs, minimizing the idle time for these vehicles, which further optimizes their energy consumption. This interconnected approach exemplifies the potential of urban environments designed around autonomous and electric mobility, heralding a revolution in urban planning and transport policy.

One of the challenges with the evolution of autonomy is the need for a reliable and robust infrastructure that supports not just individual vehicles but a network of interconnected units. This involves the deployment of high-speed data networks and robust cybersecurity measures to protect against potential threats. The influx of data from autonomous vehicles requires processing power and storage capabilities on a massive scale, urging a parallel evolution in data management and cybersecurity. The potential risks associated with autonomous vehicles, such as hacking, demand rigorous standards and innovative solutions to safeguard users' privacy and safety.

The integration of autonomous technology within the EV sector not only alters the vehicle-user interaction but also redefines business models within the automotive industry. Traditional car ownership models are giving way to new paradigms like ride-sharing and on-demand mobility services. These models thrive on autonomy, with fleets of autonomous EVs poised to meet transportation needs without the direct involvement of human drivers. Companies like Uber and Lyft are exploring autonomous fleets to enhance efficiency and profitability, signaling a shift in how transportation is consumed and perceived globally.

The regulatory landscape is another crucial factor influencing the evolution of autonomy and infrastructure. Policymakers worldwide are grappling with the complex challenge of creating a legal framework that ensures safety while fostering innovation. Regulations regarding testing, deployment, and the insurance of autonomous vehicles continue to evolve, reflecting the rapid pace of technological advancements. The establishment of these regulations is crucial in building public trust and acceptance of autonomous EVs. Regulatory environments that balance innovation with public safety will significantly influence how quickly and effectively these technologies are integrated into mainstream society.

While autonomy and infrastructure present vast possibilities, it's essential to acknowledge the roadblocks. Beyond the technological and regulatory challenges, there's the question of economic viability. The transition to a fully autonomous EV ecosystem requires substantial investment, and the economic implications for industries like insurance, logistics, and manufacturing are significant. As traditional and tech industries converge over autonomy's domain, strategic partnerships and innovative financial models will play a pivotal role in ensuring sustainable growth in this segment.

On the horizon, the evolution of autonomy and infrastructure is set to drastically transform transportation as we know it. Imagine cities where EVs autonomously navigate through interlinked grids, reducing congestion and emissions while enhancing convenience and accessibility for all. This vision, while ambitious, is becoming increasingly attainable thanks to the strides made in autonomy and infrastructure. However, it's a journey fraught with challenges requiring collaborative efforts across sectors.

For entrepreneurs and businesses venturing into the EV domain, the ongoing evolution offers a plethora of opportunities. Whether it's in developing new autonomous technologies, creating smart infrastructure, or designing innovative business models, the landscape is ripe for innovation and disruption. For forward-thinking entrepreneurs, understanding these dynamics isn't just about observing change; it's about positioning oneself to lead and benefit from this transformative era. The interplay between technology and infrastructure is more than just an advancement in mobility; it's a leap toward a sustainable, efficient, and connected future.

Chapter 16: The Global Tech Landscape

In this chapter, we journey beyond the confines of Silicon Valley to unveil the dynamic and ever-evolving global tech landscape. While Silicon Valley has long been revered as the cradle of technological innovation, other vibrant hubs around the world are emerging, reshaping the contours of this industry. From Shenzhen to Bangalore, these regions are fostering growth through unique combinations of local talent, market adaptability, and resourcefulness. Entrepreneurs and businesses are increasingly drawn to these ecosystems, not just for lower costs but for the fresh perspectives and untapped markets they offer. Yet, these opportunities come with challenges, including navigating cultural nuances, regulatory landscapes, and infrastructural barriers. As these new tech centers rise to prominence, the competition forces a reevaluation of what it takes to succeed in a globalized environment, making it imperative for entrepreneurs and innovators to adapt, learn, and thrive in ways that were unimaginable just a decade ago. The future of tech is not merely a reflection of its past; it is an amalgam of global influences shaping what will come next.

Key Players Beyond Silicon Valley

Silicon Valley is often seen as the undisputed epicenter of the tech industry. But, innovation is not confined geographically, and Silicon Valley doesn't hold a monopoly on creativity. Globally, vibrant tech ecosystems have emerged, teeming with potential and ambition. While these hubs might lack the fame of San Francisco's famed region, they're cultivating their own unique brands of innovation and influence. Indeed, it's in this expanding global landscape that we see the next chapters of the tech evolution being written.

Consider Berlin, a city once divided by political ideologies, now a unified powerhouse of technological innovation. Berlin's startup culture is characterized by a rebellious spirit—a hallmark of its tech community that thrives on diversity and a rich exchange of ideas. Entrepreneurs from around the world are attracted to its relatively affordable cost of living and its welcoming regulatory environment. The city has become a melting pot of digital nomads and ambitious founders alike, working tirelessly on game-changing ideas ranging from fintech to green energy solutions.

Across the Atlantic, in Latin America, São Paulo and Mexico City are emerging as key players in the tech world. These cities, often overshadowed in international discussions by their North American counterparts, have quietly been fostering communities that are beginning to garner attention on the world stage. In São Paulo, a burgeoning fintech scene is challenging traditional banking structures, catering to a vast population that has been historically underserved. In Mexico City, tech solutions are being integrated into sectors like transportation and communication, tapping into local needs with remarkable efficiency.

A shift towards decentralization can also be observed in the Middle East, where Tel Aviv stands out as a pivotal tech hub. Often dubbed the 'Startup Nation', Israel is home to thousands of startups, many of which are headquartered in Tel Aviv. The city is a nexus of cybersecurity, agricultural technology, and medical innovation. What makes Tel Aviv's ecosystem unique is the symbiotic relationship between its military and civilian tech sectors. This relationship drives advanced research and development, spawning innovations that often exceed what's seen in traditional civilian spheres.

Meanwhile, Nairobi, often dubbed the 'Silicon Savannah', is proving that technological ingenuity isn't limited by infrastructure shortcomings. In Kenya's capital, mobile banking solutions have redefined accessibility to financial services, transforming how business is done across the continent. Companies like M-PESA have revolutionized mobile payment platforms, providing services that cater to both the banked and unbanked populations, particularly in rural areas.

Furthermore, Bangalore, sometimes called the 'Silicon Valley of India', is a beacon of East-meets-West business synergy. Home to a high concentration of IT service companies, Bangalore's tech landscape is driven by software research, development, and export. Indian startups such as Flipkart and Ola have risen to prominence, illustrating the potential within India's market dynamics. The city is a fusion of local talent and global influence, which in turn attracts multinational technology companies, creating an ecosystem ripe for cross-border collaborations.

And then there's China, where cities like Beijing and Shenzhen are rewriting the tech playbook. With the prowess of titans like Tencent and Huawei, China's tech scene is characterized by a scale that's difficult to comprehend from a Western perspective. Shenzhen, the heart of hardware manufacturing, facilitates a pace of innovation that's dizzying. Meanwhile, Beijing is at the forefront of AI development, backed by strong governmental encouragement and vast data resources. The synergy between government policy and entrepreneurial spirit propels China's rapid technological ascent, placing it as a formidable player in global tech dynamics.

These global tech hubs exemplify that innovation can thrive anywhere, given the right mix of talent, funding, and market conditions. Each region's culture and history shape its unique approach to technology, offering different perspectives and solutions to global challenges. This diversity is vital—it's the kaleidoscope through which new ideas are born, leading to breakthroughs that can change the world.

As we continue to explore the global tech landscape, it's clear that success in technology isn't about emulating Silicon Valley. It's about leveraging local strengths and opportunities, cultivating communities that foster collaboration, and remaining open to cross-pollination of ideas from around the world. Entrepreneurs and investors alike are beginning to recognize the value in these often-overlooked markets, and in doing so, they're participating in a transformative shift towards a more inclusive and diverse tech world.

The narrative of technology and innovation is no longer a local tale—it has unfolded into a compelling global epic. The future of technology lies in this worldwide collaboration, where distinct players contribute their voices and talents to shape technological evolution in ways that are as varied as they are impactful. The challenge and opportunity lie in recognizing and nurturing these ecosystems beyond the glare of Silicon Valley, allowing for a broader narrative of innovation to emerge, resonating across continents and cultures.

Emerging Markets and Challenges

The global tech landscape is no longer confined to the well-trodden paths of Silicon Valley. Emerging markets offer fertile ground for innovative pursuits, often characterized by youthful demographics, burgeoning middle classes, and untapped potential. Within these diverse ecosystems, challenges abound. Yet, for the savvy entrepreneur, these challenges are opportunities in disguise. They force businesses to think creatively, adapt rapidly, and build sustainable models that can withstand unique market pressures.

Consider Asia, where rapid urbanization fuels a thirst for technological solutions. Cities are evolving into smart cities, driven by the need for efficient public transport, waste management, and energy distribution. This transformation presents immense opportunities for tech startups. However, penetrating these markets requires more than just innovative products. It demands an understanding of local cultures, regulations, and infrastructures. Navigating these complexities can prove daunting for companies used to homogenous consumer bases.

Africa, often dubbed the 'last frontier' for tech innovation, offers equally challenging terrains. Internet connectivity and digital infrastructure can be inconsistent, yet the continent boasts the fastest-growing population of young, tech-savvy users. Mobile technology has already revolutionized sectors like banking, and there remains a vast potential for other industries. Here lies the paradox: the market is rich with opportunities, yet infrastructure inadequacies can stymie progress. Entrepreneurs need to be agile, finding solutions that work within these limitations rather than against them.

Latin America's tech scene is blossoming, driven by increased access to education and a surge in tech-based entrepreneurship. Countries like Brazil and Mexico are becoming tech hubs, with startups tackling problems from financial inclusion to healthcare access. Yet, political instability and economic fluctuations can introduce unpredictability, disrupting business operations. Companies here must be resilient, employing strategies that allow for rapid pivots and flexible growth plans.

With emerging markets come distinctive consumer behaviors and preferences. Entrepreneurs must tailor their approaches, offering products and services that resonate with local needs. In India, for example, consumers' emphasis on affordability and functionality has driven successful tech innovations in the affordable smartphone market. Startups looking to capture these audiences need a deep understanding of local economies and spending habits.

The regulatory environment adds another layer of complexity. In some emerging markets, tech regulations are still evolving, creating uncertainty for startups. Entrepreneurs must navigate these fluid landscapes, often finding themselves in dialogue with policymakers. While this can slow down progress, it also offers startups a unique opportunity: to help shape the very regulations that govern their industries, thereby paving the way for smoother operations in the future.

An often overlooked challenge is talent acquisition. Emerging markets may have a wealth of potential, but building a skilled workforce takes time. Entrepreneurs need to invest in education and training to develop the talent they need. Partnering with local universities or setting up in-house training programs can build a pipeline of skilled professionals, essential for supporting growth and innovation.

The allure of emerging markets is undeniable, yet the path to success is fraught with risks. Entrepreneurs must embrace a mindset of experimentation, learning, and adaptation. They must be willing to "fail fast" and iterate, using failures as stepping stones to refine their strategies and improve their offerings. This resilience, combined with a deep understanding of local contexts, can transform obstacles into catalysts for growth.

Moreover, entrepreneurs should leverage networks and communities. Local partnerships can provide invaluable insights and footholds in the market, offering resources and support that would be hard to obtain independently. Aligning with local stakeholders not only facilitates entry into the market but also fosters goodwill and a sense of shared purpose.

With every challenge comes the promise of innovation. Whether it's developing infrastructure solutions in Africa or devising regulatory frameworks that encourage tech entrepreneurship in Asia, the potential for growth is immense. For entrepreneurs, these emerging markets are not just places to do business but rather arenas that test their resilience and capacity to drive meaningful change.

In the end, the story of tech in emerging markets is a story of the future. It's where innovation meets necessity, where entrepreneurs redefine what's possible, and where the next generation of tech giants may very well rise. As the lines between global and local blur, the need to think globally while acting locally becomes paramount. It's in these dynamic environments that entrepreneurs will write the next chapter of the tech narrative, shaping a more inclusive, diverse, and innovative global tech landscape.

Chapter 17: Navigating Economic Downturns

Economic downturns can hit with the suddenness of a summer storm, leaving both budding and seasoned entrepreneurs grappling for a sturdy foothold. In the fast-paced world of tech startups, resilience isn't just a desirable trait; it's a crucial survival tool. Learning to navigate these tumultuous times involves a keen understanding of market dynamics combined with the ability to pivot quickly while safeguarding your core vision. Entrepreneurs need to draw lessons from history, analyzing how past innovators not only weathered recessions but emerged stronger and more agile. By integrating fiscal prudence with innovative resilience, businesses can transform apparent threats into opportunities for growth. This often means recalibrating strategies, optimizing resources, and reinforcing the adaptability of the workforce. The journey through economic shifts is less about mere survival and more about redefining success to include tenacity, courage, and a deep commitment to innovation.

Surviving Recessions and Market Shifts

In the life cycle of any business, economic downturns are as inevitable as the turning of the seasons. Yet, throughout history, some companies have not only managed to survive these turbulent times but have emerged stronger. The ability to navigate these financial tempests can often be the defining factor between success and failure in the startup ecosystem. For entrepreneurs and those involved in tech industries, understanding and anticipating market shifts isn't just advantageous—it's essential.

Recessions, though daunting, can serve as crucibles. They test the resilience, adaptability, and innovation of a company, forging businesses that are more robust and finely tuned to the needs of their clientele. The core of surviving these periods lies in one's mindset and strategic approach. Are you prepared to pivot, to reassess your assets, and to make bold decisions that steer your company through the stormy waters?

Consider the story of Apple in the late 1990s. On the brink of bankruptcy, the company made decisive moves that later cemented its dominance in the tech world. Apple's leadership focused on innovation and design excellence, decisions that initially seemed risky but eventually paid off in spades. The introduction of the iMac and iPod revolutionized how consumers engaged with technology. These moves illustrate that crises can lead to opportunities if companies are willing to adapt and innovate.

When faced with recession, it's crucial to evaluate your core value propositions. Ask yourself: what unique aspects of your product or service resonate most with your audience? Many businesses find strength in diversification, expanding their offerings to cater to new markets or customer needs. For instance, during economic slowdowns, a company primarily focused on enterprise solutions might pivot to offer scaled-down versions of their products to small businesses seeking cost-effective alternatives. This agility can help maintain revenue streams and even capture market share from struggling competitors.

Cash flow management during a recession becomes the lifeblood of a startup. Cutting unnecessary costs, optimizing operational efficiencies, and carefully managing resources can determine whether a business sinks or swims. However, cost-cutting alone is not the answer. It's about strategic allocation of resources to areas that will yield the highest returns or ensure long-term sustainability. Investing in technology that automates and streamlines operations can dramatically improve productivity and output without proportional increases in cost.

Equally important is maintaining a transparent and open line of communication with stakeholders, including investors, employees, and customers. Trust becomes invaluable during times of uncertainty. When stakeholders understand the rationale behind tough decisions, like downsizing or restructuring, they're more likely to offer the support and patience needed for the company's recovery. This transparency builds stronger relationships that can support long-term growth beyond the crises.

History also shows us that downturns can level the playing field for startups against established giants. As resources become constrained, even larger corporations must adjust, often unveiling gaps or inefficiencies in their operations that nimble startups can exploit. These times of chaos can potentially open pathways to enter new market segments or capitalizing on emerging trends that larger, less agile competitors may overlook.

Another strategic maneuver in surviving recessions is focusing on *customer retention*. Acquiring new customers during a recession is challenging and costly. Instead, businesses should aim to solidify their existing customer base by enhancing customer experiences, improving service or product quality, and offering loyalty rewards. A satisfied customer base not only ensures consistent revenue but also can serve as a potent source of word-of-mouth marketing.

Reflecting on past economic downturns, such as the 2008 financial crisis or the more recent COVID-19 pandemic, we learn that preparedness coupled with a proactive approach allows startups and companies to weather the storm. Many who thrived during these times were those who viewed crises not as insurmountable obstacles but as opportunities for reinvention and growth.

Entrepreneurs must also engage in scenario planning—anticipating various outcomes and devising strategies for each possibility. While it may seem impractical to predict all variables of a recession, understanding potential risks and preparing for them provides a strategic advantage. This planning enables quick decision-making when markets take unexpected turns, allowing businesses to transition smoothly amid the chaos.

The tech industry, more than any other, experiences rapid cycles of boom and bust. However, these cycles also illustrate the importance of resilient planning and calculated risk-taking. Founders and executives must internalize the idea that adaptability and forward-thinking are just as critical as immediate profitability. Encouraging a company culture that embraces experimentation, learning, and growth-oriented strategies can turn market shifts into learning opportunities, reinforcing the foundation for future success.

In conclusion, surviving a recession and market shift is an amalgamation of strategically leveraging resources, enhancing innovation, fostering strong relationships, and maintaining a nimble business model. Those who emerge triumphant are not just prepared for challenges but are adept at turning them into stepping stones towards long-term success. In the ever-evolving landscape of the tech industry, this ability to adapt and evolve isn't just beneficial—it's transformative.

Lessons from Past Crises

Crises are often unforeseen, striking at the heart of economies and businesses with little warning. Yet, as disruptive as they are, they also bring invaluable insights for those willing to learn. Examining past economic downturns reveals patterns and lessons that can be crucial for entrepreneurs in the tech industry and beyond. From these past crises, we extract wisdom to navigate future challenges with greater resilience and foresight.

The early 2000s dot-com bust is perhaps one of the most significant lessons for today's tech entrepreneurs. As investments soared in the late 1990s, fueled by a belief in limitless potential of the internet, startups flourished. Entrepreneurs enjoyed access to seemingly endless venture capital. But the bubble burst, leading to massive losses and a stark reminder of the risks associated with overvaluation and speculation. This era taught us the importance of sustainable growth over rapid, blind expansion. Businesses with solid fundamentals endured, while those built solely on hype faded away.

Another stark lesson from the dot-com era is the necessity for tangible value creation. The exuberance of the internet boom led many to launch companies with no clear revenue model or understanding of market needs. In hindsight, it's clear that a viable business model is non-negotiable. For entrepreneurs today, the message is simple: innovative ideas must be anchored in reality. Offering a product or service that meets genuine needs ensures longevity beyond market fluctuations.

In the immediate aftermath of the bust, there was also a remarkable shift in how businesses approached innovation and investment. Companies that survived began focusing more on customer-centric processes and ensuring operational efficiency. This reevaluation of priorities teaches us the power of adaptability and the importance of refining business models in response to changing market conditions.

The 2008 financial crisis offers another perspective. The collapse of major financial institutions and plunging global markets demonstrated the interconnectedness of industries and the far-reaching impacts of financial oversight failures. In the tech industry, this crisis taught entrepreneurs the need for financial prudence and the dangers of outsized leverage. It was a wake-up call for startups to maintain robust financial health and build solid cash reserves, lessons that remain vital today.

Integrity and trust also emerged as crucial components during economic distress. The mistrust in financial systems during the 2008 crisis highlighted how vulnerable businesses could be to reputational damage. For tech entrepreneurs, preserving stakeholder trust through transparency and ethical practices can make the difference not just in surviving a downturn, but in thriving beyond it. Long-term credibility is an asset, one that tech startups must nurture vigilantly.

A more recent example is the COVID-19 pandemic, which underscored the volatility that external forces can introduce. The rapid digital transformation spurred by pandemic restrictions highlighted the potential for adaptability. Companies that pivoted quickly, embracing remote work and digital services, often came out stronger. This period taught tech entrepreneurs the importance of agility—not just in technology, but in mindset and strategy.

Moreover, the pandemic emphasized the importance of diversified revenue streams. Firms overly dependent on a single market or product line faced tremendous pressure. Diversification emerges as a protective shield, enabling businesses to weather sector-specific downturns. Entrepreneurs today would do well to incorporate this lesson, establishing multiple pathways for revenue generation and innovation.

The nature of crises also reveals the importance of having a robust network. During downturns, startups often find themselves relying on connections for guidance, partnerships, and financial assistance. Building and maintaining a strong network of mentors, investors, and industry peers provides not just business opportunities, but a wealth of shared knowledge and resources that are critical during tough times.

Resilience is the ultimate lesson drawn from past crises. Resilience doesn't just mean enduring or weathering a storm; it means adapting, learning, and evolving with every challenge. This mindset of resilience fosters environments where creativity flourishes and innovation thrives even when faced with adversity. It's about cultivating a culture within organizations that empowers teams to tackle obstacles with a positive and proactive approach.

Understanding and internalizing these lessons elevates entrepreneurs beyond survival to a state where they are prepared to seize new opportunities as they arise. History shows us that while crises may be inevitable, the companies that learn from them—and pivot accordingly—are not only more likely to endure, but also to pave the path forward into a more robust future. Embracing these historical lessons allows today's tech entrepreneurs to navigate economic downturns with strategic confidence and renewed hope for what lies beyond the horizon.

Chapter 18: Leadership in Tech

At the heart of tech innovation lies a distinct breed of leadership that demands not only technical acumen but also a visionary approach to navigating ever-shifting landscapes. Visionary leaders in tech are those who see beyond the immediate, envisioning futures that others might deem impossible. They inspire teams to push the boundaries of what's possible, blending bold ideas with pragmatic execution. These leaders understand that managing growth transcends mere expansion; it's about fostering an adaptable culture that thrives amidst change and transition. Their impact is often felt in how they turn audacious ideas into tangible realities, encouraging calculated risk-taking while aligning mission-driven goals with sustainable practices. Such leadership paves the way for breakthroughs, accordingly transforming individual enterprises into pivotal forces within the global tech ecosystem.

Visionary Leaders and Their Impact

The digital age has borne witness to a cascade of technological transformations, each spearheaded by leaders with audacious visions. These leaders didn't just stumble upon success; they meticulously charted paths that disrupted existing paradigms and ushered in novel ways of living and working. As we delve into their stories, one thing becomes clear: visionary leaders in tech are not merely managers of resources but architects of the future. Their impact, profound and far-reaching, is a testament to the power of visionary thinking.

Steve Jobs, for example, wasn't just a CEO; he was a maestro orchestrating a symphony of innovation and design. Under his leadership, Apple blossomed into an icon of innovation, rewriting the rules of personal computing, communication, and even entertainment. Jobs had a knack for identifying potential where others saw only limitations. He believed in blending technology with artistry, making products that were not only functional but also aesthetically desirable. His vision birthed products like the iPod, iPhone, and iPad, devices that have become integral to modern life. In so doing, he didn't just create products; he changed how we interact with technology on a daily basis.

This kind of visionary thinking wasn't limited to Western shores. Jack Ma, the charismatic founder of Alibaba, also exemplifies the hallmark of a visionary leader. Rising from humble beginnings in China, Ma dared to dream of a digital marketplace that would connect Chinese enterprises to the world. The odds were against him, with skeptics quick to doubt the viability of his vision. Yet, Ma's unwavering commitment to his vision transformed Alibaba into a global e-commerce powerhouse. His belief in the potential of the internet to democratize commerce illustrates how visionary leadership can transcend geographical and cultural boundaries, fostering economic opportunities on a global scale.

Elon Musk takes the narrative of visionary leadership to a whole new dimension—literally and figuratively. With SpaceX, Tesla, and Neuralink, Musk isn't just reshaping industries; he's redefining what humankind believes is possible. His ventures push the limits of space travel, electric vehicles, and even human cognition. Musk's willingness to embrace radical challenges, often against conventional wisdom, shows the power of setting and pursuing ambitious goals. By targeting Mars as a future destination and advancing the sustainability of Earth's ecosystems, Musk embodies a rare breed of leadership that not only aims for commercial success but also grapples with profound existential questions.

There's a pattern that resonates through the stories of these leaders: the fusion of personal passion with a deep understanding of market trends and technological capabilities. Visionary leaders aren't just risk-takers; they're keen observers and learners who adapt rapidly to change. Satya Nadella's leadership of Microsoft represents another compelling case, highlighting the importance of humility and learning in leadership. Nadella transitioned Microsoft towards cloud computing, prioritizing innovation and a growth mindset within one of the world's largest companies. By fostering a culture of empathy and collaboration, Nadella leveraged his vision to reinvigorate Microsoft's stance in the tech industry.

However, visionary leadership isn't without its challenges. Such leaders often navigate a landscape rife with skepticism and resistance. Resilient and adaptive, these individuals persist through criticism, learning and iterating as they go. A significant aspect of their impact lies in their ability to inspire and galvanize their teams—cultivating an environment that embraces creativity and pushes boundaries. These leaders possess a thorough understanding that the realization of their vision depends on nurturing talent and building robust ecosystems that translate individual brilliance into collective achievement.

The impact of visionary leaders is multidimensional. On an economic level, the companies they build often become substantial contributors to their local and global economies, creating jobs and driving technological advancement. Socially, they redefine societal norms and values, often blazing the trail for diversity, inclusion, and ethical considerations in technology development. Culturally, their work influences art, media, and the very way people perceive and engage with the world.

Visionary leaders also bear the responsibility of addressing ethical dilemmas that come with technological advancements. As AI and biotechnology advance, leaders need to align innovation with humanity's best interests, ensuring the ethical deployment of new technologies. Those who understand this balance can set a precedent for future innovations that prioritize not just profit, but societal well-being. It's through this lens that the true impact of visionary leadership is most profoundly felt—not only in their immediate innovations but also in their enduring legacy on the world.

In conclusion, the story of visionary leaders is one of courage, foresight, and relentless pursuit of a better tomorrow. These leaders challenge us to reimagine what's possible, inspiring entire generations to dream bigger and aim higher. Their impact extends beyond market caps and technological advancements; they reshape the very fabric of society. As the tech industry continues to evolve, it will be these individuals—imbued with vision and passion—who will drive the next wave of transformative change. The world waits, ready to be reshaped once again by those audacious enough to imagine it differently.

Managing Growth and Transition

Leadership in the tech industry demands more than just an innovative idea or a technological breakthrough. It requires the ability to manage growth and navigate transitions with precision and foresight. The landscape of tech companies is littered with stories of rapid rises followed by dramatic falls, often because growth outpaced the ability to manage it.

To successfully lead a tech company through growth phases, it's critical to understand that growth brings new challenges. These challenges aren't just about scaling operations, but also about maintaining a coherent vision and culture amidst the chaos. When a startup begins to scale, it transforms from a small, tight-knit team into a larger organization where communication can become strained, and maintaining the original innovative spirit can be difficult.

One of the fundamental aspects of managing growth in tech is hiring. As teams expand, it's imperative to hire not only for skills but also for cultural fit. The people who thrived in the scrappy, resource-limited days might not have the same impact within a more structured, larger organization. Balancing experience with fresh perspectives is key, ensuring that the organization doesn't become too rigid but also doesn't lose its edge.

Another critical factor is scaling infrastructure. As user bases expand, technologies that worked during the startup phase may start to buckle under pressure. Leaders need to anticipate these shifts and invest in scalable solutions early. This might involve transitioning from in-house servers to cloud-based services or redesigning the architecture of a product to handle more data and concurrent users.

Leadership during periods of significant growth must also include a robust feedback mechanism. As a company grows, the distance between its leaders and its frontline employees often widens. Leaders need to create channels where feedback is encouraged and acted upon, ensuring that they remain attuned to the ground realities even while looking at the bigger picture. This helps in maintaining an inclusive culture where every employee feels valued and heard.

Transitioning from a startup to a larger company also requires a shift in strategic thinking. Short-term goals, which might have been the focus during the early days, need to be aligned with long-term visions. Leaders must articulate clear roadmaps that not only keep the team aligned but also entice investors and stakeholders by showcasing sustainable growth paths.

Leadership in tech also involves being agile and adaptable. Market conditions can change rapidly, and what worked yesterday might not work tomorrow. It's necessary for leaders to build adaptable business models that can pivot when necessary without losing sight of the core vision. Flexibility in leadership can mean the difference between thriving and floundering in the face of unexpected challenges.

Moreover, managing growth requires being prepared for potential setbacks. Leaders must be pragmatic and anticipate downturns, competitive threats, and regulatory challenges. Having contingency plans and being proactive in addressing risks before they escalate is part of the resilience a tech leader must develop.

One of the most underrated aspects of leading through growth is ensuring ethical practices are embedded in every level of the organization. As the company expands, its impact on society and its responsibilities grow as well. Leaders have to set standards of ethics and compliance that lead by example, ensuring that rapid growth doesn't come at the expense of ethical compromises.

Lastly, managing growth involves celebrating the wins to keep team morale high. Growth doesn't only mean new pressures; it means successes, achievements, and benchmarks surpassed. Leaders must recognize these moments and celebrate them in ways that reinforce company values and inspire teams to continue striving for excellence.

In the whirlwind of tech expansion, leaders who master the delicate dance of managing growth and transition not only steer their companies towards success but also set benchmarks for others to follow. The art of balancing vision with execution, innovation with infrastructure, and growth with sustainability is what distinguishes the true visionaries in the tech world.

Chapter 19: The Importance of Company Culture

The success of any startup often hinges not just on its groundbreaking idea but on the intangible yet impactful asset of company culture. It's more than just a set of values displayed on a wall—it's the essence that binds the team together, igniting passion and innovation from within. When leaders define and embody values that resonate with their team, they're establishing a blueprint for behavior and decision-making that aligns with long-term goals. This cultural blueprint can cultivate an environment where creativity thrives, challenges are met with resilience, and everyone, from the intern to the CEO, feels empowered to contribute their best. In a landscape as competitive and fast-paced as the tech industry, a strong, well-aligned company culture can be the differentiator that propels a startup not only to survive but to transform into a leader that continuously adapts and innovates. Thus, cultivating the right culture isn't just a business strategy; it's a commitment to sustaining a legacy of success and impact.

Defining Values and Practices

Values and practices are more than just words molded into a mission statement or slogans peppered across the walls of an office. They're the backbone of what gives a company its unique identity and determines its path to success or failure. In the tech industry, where innovation moves at light speed, defining these core elements with clarity and precision is non-negotiable. Entrepreneurs often find themselves at crossroads, pondering what will make their fledgling startups soar among giants. It's in these moments that a well-defined company culture, rooted in authentic values and practical practices, becomes the compass guiding them through turbulent seas.

At the heart of defining values and practices is the simple yet profound notion of purpose. Startups that succeed aren't just chasing profits; they're on a mission to solve a problem or fill a void in the universe. Look at the most transformative tech companies—each began with a fundamental question or a vexing problem that needed a solution. This quest is what shapes their values and informs the practices that underpin their day-to-day operations. Imagine a startup that aims to democratize education through technology; its values might emphasize accessibility, inclusivity, and lifelong learning. By embedding these values in the fabric of the company, every decision, from hiring to product design, reflects this overarching purpose.

Defining clear values early on isn't just inspirational; it's strategic. As companies grow, their core beliefs guide decision-making processes and even transcend the presence of individual leaders. In turbulent times, these core values serve as the sturdy framework within which appropriate actions can be measured and executed. Take Google, for instance, whose informal motto, "Don't be evil," served as a moral compass, influencing countless decisions and fostering a culture of ethical innovation. While the complexities of growth have tested and evolved Google's applications of this motto, the initial clarity set a tone that resonated deeply with employees and users alike.

Creating practices that breathe life into these values is where the real alchemy happens. It's one thing to claim a value like "innovation" or "customer-centricity," but another to embed it into everyday activity. Let's talk about meetings, a fundamental part of business life. A practice inspired by a commitment to efficiency and respect might include limiting meeting times to 30 minutes. This simple rule not only fosters productivity but also aligns with a company value of valuing employees' time. In a world where work can easily become transactional, practices like these ensure values become lived experiences rather than lofty ideals.

Given the dynamic landscape of the tech industry, flexibility in shaping and reshaping these practices is crucial. Companies must avoid the trap of viewing their cultural framework as immutable. As the external environment evolves, so too should internal practices. Netflix, for instance, revolutionized the concept of HR practices with its "Freedom and Responsibility" culture deck, fostering an environment that valued performance over effort and individual initiative over stringent processes. This adaptive approach allowed them to respond with agility in a rapidly changing market.

Essential to embedding values are leaders who exemplify them. Leadership in any organization sets the precedent for how seriously values are taken. When leaders walk the talk, it sends a powerful message to every rung of the corporate ladder. It solidifies trust and engages employees in a manner that transcends the mundane transactions that can characterize corporate work. Additionally, hiring processes that evaluate candidates based not only on skills but also on alignment with company values can create a cohesive organic culture that doesn't need to be constantly policed.

Tech giants and startups alike can't afford to overlook the power of story in defining and communicating values. Stories that illustrate company values in action—whether it's an anecdote from the CEO or a testimonial from an employee—are invaluable. Narrative-driven cultural understandings don't just educate; they inspire and stick. They allow employees to visualize their roles within the company's larger mission, cultivating an internal community of brand ambassadors eager to advocate externally as well.

Moreover, authenticity in defining these values can't be overstated. It's not just about crafting a narrative that looks attractive in a recruitment drive or to investors; the walk has to match the talk. Empty rhetoric is easily exposed, especially in today's digital age where transparency is demanded by stakeholders at all fronts. Companies that say one thing but live another quickly lose credibility, both internally and externally, which can lead to disengagement, attrition, and reputational damage.

As we delve deeper into the tech startup ecosystem, let's remember that the companies defining tomorrow's landscapes are those adept at balancing solid, unwavering values with evolving, adaptable practices. Every decision, every product launch, every pivot backed by clearly defined values becomes a step further toward a well-aligned, purpose-driven future in the sprawling terrain of technological advancement. The innovation that matters is innovation grounded in authenticity, fueled by passion, and guided by an unwavering sense of purpose.

In conclusion, as startups and seasoned enterprises alike continue to navigate the choppy waters of technological evolution, they must steer towards a destination defined by their core values and carefully cultivated practices. What's at stake is not just their own success but also their legacy in an ever-evolving industry. It's a compass of principles and protocols that, when set aright, will carry their ventures from the formative days of launch to the unpredictable landscapes of future frontiers.

Aligning Culture with Long-Term Goals

In the fast-paced world of technology and startups, the significance of company culture extends far beyond casual Fridays and open office layouts. Aligning culture with long-term goals is crucial for ensuring that a company not only survives but thrives over time. This alignment serves as the rudder guiding a company through the unchartered waters of innovation and market shifts. With a harmonious cultural compass, startups can navigate challenges with a unified sense of purpose and direction.

Organizations that successfully harmonize their culture with their long-term objectives often enjoy a more cohesive work environment. Employees know not just what they are working on, but why their work matters. This clarity can be incredibly motivating and keeps teams aligned with the broader vision of the company. Without this alignment, a company risks competing priorities that can lead to fragmentation and inefficiency.

The process of aligning culture with long-term goals begins with clearly defining the company's values and mission. Startup leaders must communicate these values consistently and authentically. When employees understand and share in these principles, they are more likely to contribute meaningfully towards achieving strategic objectives. This alignment isn't just about top-down directives; it's about creating an inclusive atmosphere where employees feel their contributions are part of a larger mission.

A key strategy for achieving this cultural alignment is through active engagement and open communication. Regular meetings, feedback sessions, and forums for employee voices encourage an ongoing dialogue between management and staff. This not only helps in fine-tuning the company's direction but also fosters a sense of belonging, where every team member feels responsible for and committed to the organization's success.

Moreover, leaders play a pivotal role in embodying and reinforcing the company culture. They must model the behaviors and attitudes they wish to see throughout the organization. Whether it's prioritizing work-life balance or championing diversity and inclusion, leaders set the standard. Their actions serve as a benchmark for what is expected and valued, thus steering the cultural ethos of the company towards its envisioned future.

However, the journey to aligning culture with long-term goals is not without its challenges. Startups in particular face the dual pressures of rapid scaling and maintaining their foundational culture. The initial "move fast and break things" mentality may serve a young company well, but as it grows, a culture that supports sustained innovation and resilience becomes necessary. Transitioning the culture without losing its core can be a delicate balance to achieve.

An adaptive culture can facilitate this balance. By encouraging a mindset that embraces change, companies can remain agile. Employees who see change as an opportunity rather than a threat can better support the company's evolution. This adaptability needs to be ingrained into the culture through continuous learning and development opportunities that prepare employees for tomorrow's challenges.

In the end, aligning culture with long-term goals is about establishing a shared vision that resonates with everyone in the organization. When done effectively, it cultivates a culture of excellence where goals are not just met but exceeded. The culture acts as a guiding light, informing strategic decisions and empowering teams to contribute their best work. As we've seen with successful tech giants, culture and strategy must go hand-in-hand to achieve lasting impact.

Ultimately, this alignment is foundational to building a sustainable organization. A well-aligned culture can become a competitive advantage, attracting top talent and fostering innovation. It becomes embedded in the way the company reacts to unforeseen challenges, how it services its customers, and how it plans for the future. When a company achieves this cultural alignment, it's not just prepared for the journey ahead—it's primed to redefine it.

The lessons learned from aligning culture with long-term goals reiterate the importance of intentionality in building and nurturing company culture. It's about crafting a narrative that everyone in the company not only understands but feels a part of. This inclusion is what turns aspirations into achievements, fostering a legacy that stands the test of time. As we continue exploring the intricate dynamics of success within the tech industry, it becomes clearer that culture isn't just a backdrop—it's a driving force.

Chapter 20: Mergers and Acquisitions

Mergers and acquisitions have long been critical strategies for growth and expansion in the tech landscape, offering startups a pathway to scale swiftly and established companies a means to stay ahead of competitors. These high-stakes decisions often reflect a delicate balance of risk and reward, where astute assessments of market trends, technological synergies, and cultural fit can dictate the difference between a transformative merger and an ill-fated takeover. Successful cases highlight the catalytic precision with which industry leaders pinpoint complementarities—just as Google did with Android, envisioning the smartphone's vast potential or Facebook's acquisition of Instagram, which unlocked unprecedented social media engagement. Conversely, high-profile failures, such as AOL's ill-fated merger with Time Warner, serve as cautionary chronicles of strategic misalignment and cultural discord. Understanding these dynamics provides entrepreneurs and stakeholders with invaluable insights, urging them to approach M&A not merely as financial maneuvers but as deeply strategic decisions foundational to enduring innovation and success in the ever-evolving tech ecosystem.

Strategies for Growth and Expansion

As the technology landscape constantly evolves, the phrase "grow or perish" couldn't be more apt. In the relentless drive to dominate markets, mergers and acquisitions (M&A) emerge as pivotal strategies for growth and expansion. They aren't merely business transactions; they're transformative forces that reshape industries, redefine futures, and create value in ways that organic growth often can't accomplish alone.

For many entrepreneurs, M&As represent a tantalizing shortcut to market leadership. They allow companies to leapfrog hurdles, acquire essential technologies, or even assimilate talent pools that could propel them past the competition. Integrating a rival or a complementary firm demands not only a strategic vision but a courageous appetite for risk and a deep understanding of the financial landscape.

Let's delve into how tech startups, particularly in Silicon Valley, have leveraged this strategy. Consider the acquisition of a small startup offering a revolutionary technology or service. The buying company not only absorbs innovation but concurrently eliminates a potential competitor. This isn't about stifling competition; it's about harnessing synergy. Companies that understand this create new ecosystems that foster growth and innovation at an unprecedented scale.

It's important to recognize that successful M&A strategies are rooted in a deep comprehension of one's own strengths and weaknesses. Companies with a strong understanding of their core competencies can identify strategic targets that will bolster their capabilities. For instance, if a company excels in software but lacks hardware expertise, acquiring a hardware firm can fill that gap, offering a fuller product suite to consumers.

One major advantage of M&As is speed. Building a new area of expertise internally can take years, which is a luxury few companies can afford in today's fast-paced tech environment. Acquiring a firm that already excels in this area can instantly bolster a company's prowess, allowing it to keep pace with or outmaneuver the competition.

However, not all M&As lead to success. The intricacies of blending different corporate cultures can unravel even the most promising mergers. Companies must carefully align cultures and values to fully realize synergies. Without this, employee morale can plummet, leading to talent drain and inefficiencies that can erode anticipated benefits.

To prevent such pitfalls, clear communication and a solid integration plan become paramount. This involves establishing shared goals from the outset and ensuring that all teams are moving toward a common objective. Often, this requires a dedicated integration team that manages the nuances of blending diverse workforces and operational styles.

Moreover, understanding the market landscape is crucial. Identifying not just current demands, but also future trends allows firms to make acquisitions that position them strategically for long-term growth. Predictive analytics and market research can offer insights, but intuition and visionary leadership frequently play an equally critical role.

A case in point is Google's acquisition of YouTube back in 2006. At the time, video was not yet the dominant force it is today. Google recognized the potential of video content and its capacity to attract massive audiences. By acquiring YouTube, they not only entered the burgeoning video sharing market but became a leading figure in digital advertising.

Risk, however, always accompanies power moves. There's an inherent gamble in M&As, stemming from market fluctuations or unexpected shifts in consumer behavior. Due diligence procedures must be exhaustive, examining financials, legal standings, patents, and even consumer sentiments. The more comprehensive the foresight, the more effectively a company can mitigate risk.

Yet, it's not just about minimizing risk—sometimes, the bravest choices yield the brightest futures. Companies that embrace unconventional mergers often do so with an entrepreneurial spirit. They seek not just to expand their market share, but to transform industries, redefine possibilities, and even catalyze entire technological revolutions.

Ultimately, Mergers and Acquisitions serve as a testament to the belief in potential—what a company can become and achieve. Entrepreneurs at the helm of these strategic maneuvers need the acuity to recognize opportunity amidst ambiguity. As they venture down this path, they're not merely crafting business deals, but reshaping the future of the tech industry itself.

The narrative of growth through M&As in the tech industry, therefore, is not just one of assimilation, but of creation. It's about unifying diverse threads into a coherent tapestry capable of weaving the future. While strategies, challenges, and outcomes may vary, the essence of growth remains constant: the unyielding pursuit of what lies beyond the horizon.

Successful and Failed Case Studies

Mergers and acquisitions (M&A) have long woven the tapestry of the business world, serving as both harbingers of growth and cataclysms of failure. For entrepreneurs, business students, and tech enthusiasts, analyzing these stories provides insights into the mechanics of innovation and the harsh realities of the market. Some mergers serve as masterclasses in synergy, turning separate entities into formidable giants, while others offer cautionary tales of overambition and mismatched cultures.

One of the most iconic success stories in tech M&A is the acquisition of YouTube by Google in 2006 for $1.65 billion. At that time, YouTube was a fledgling platform, burgeoning with potential but lacking the resources for explosive growth. Google saw the immense opportunity in video content long before it became omnipresent. By leveraging Google's infrastructure and resources, YouTube transformed from a niche startup to the world's largest video platform. This acquisition was not only about a financial transaction but also about strategically integrating technology, which encouraged viewer engagement in a rapidly changing digital landscape.

Contrast this with the acquisition of MySpace by News Corp in 2005 for $580 million. MySpace was initially well-positioned to dominate social media. However, the integration did not align well with MySpace's culture and user base, which was more tech-savvy than the traditional publishing mindset of News Corp. Over time, a series of missteps in strategy and a lack of innovation compared to emerging competitors like Facebook led to MySpace's precipitous decline. This case underscores the importance of cultural alignment and forward-thinking leadership in M&A.

Facebook's acquisition of Instagram in 2012 is another success story that illustrates the power of capturing emerging trends. At the time, Instagram was a small, stylish app prized for its photo-sharing capabilities and rapidly growing user base. For $1 billion, Facebook effectively neutralized a potential competitor and reinforced its dominance in social media. The wisdom of this move is evident today as Instagram continues to grow robustly, eventually becoming one of Facebook's most significant assets.

On the other hand, AOL's acquisition of Time Warner in 2000 represents one of the most famous failed mergers in history. Valued at $165 billion, this merger was meant to combine old media with the new internet frontier, creating synergies across television, internet services, and magazines. However, cultural clashes, combined with an overestimation of synergies and a lack of cohesive vision, led to its collapse. The dot-com bubble burst shortly after the merger, further compounding the financial strain. This case vividly illustrates how external market conditions and internal misalignments can derail even the most promising deals.

Occasionally, mergers and acquisitions offer unexpected lessons in resilience and strategic pivoting. Consider Microsoft's acquisition of LinkedIn in 2016 for $26.2 billion. At the time, many were skeptical. However, Microsoft's strategic integration of LinkedIn's professional network into its own suite of productivity tools, like Microsoft Office, capitalized on the professional-centric data LinkedIn possessed. This acquisition has since been deemed successful, illustrating how a clear vision for integration and synergy can produce lasting value.

Yet, not all stories of successful M&A survive the test of time unchanged. When HP acquired Palm in 2010, it aimed to enter the smartphone market with Palm's promising WebOS platform, marking a significant move in tech history. Unfortunately, this venture was ultimately unsuccessful. HP's inability to effectively market WebOS and its delayed entry into an already competitive smartphone space led to the project's discontinuation in less than two years. This misstep highlights the critical factor of timing and the importance of proper market positioning.

Furthermore, the acquisition of Skype by eBay for $2.6 billion in 2005 unveils the complexities of M&A misalignment. The goal was to complement eBay's online auction platform with Skype's communication capabilities. However, the intended synergies didn't fructify, leading eBay to sell a majority stake of Skype to private investors a few years later. The missed opportunity lay in the lack of integration vision, which eBay underestimated.

An instructive contrast appears in Amazon's acquisition of Whole Foods in 2017 for $13.7 billion. This merger melded the worlds of e-commerce and brick-and-mortar retail, representing Amazon's strategic endeavor to enhance its grocery business. By leveraging Whole Foods' established brand and physical infrastructure along with Amazon's logistics and technological prowess, the acquisition enabled rapid delivery innovations like Amazon Fresh, showcasing a winning alignment of operational capabilities.

Every merger or acquisition encapsulates a unique narrative shaped by strategic foresight or the lack thereof. The success of acquisitions doesn't merely rely on financial calculations but profoundly on vision, timing, and cultural symmetry. Each case offers volumes of insight: successful integrations reveal how businesses can leverage new strengths, while failures dissect the seams of fractured strategies. As the M&A landscape evolves, these historical case studies serve to guide current and future leaders in making informed and strategic decisions.

Ultimately, successful mergers and acquisitions teach lessons in adaptability, resilience, and seeing beyond the numbers. They bear testament to the infinite possibilities that emerge when innovation meets opportunity. Conversely, the failures remind us vigorously about the pitfalls of complacency, mismatched objectives, and the relentless challenge of sustaining growth amidst disruption. Entrepreneurs, students, and industry insiders can glean vital insights by immersing themselves in these narratives, equipping them with the foresight and wisdom to navigate the complex terrain of modern business.

Chapter 21: The Role of Government Regulation

In the constantly shifting landscape of technology and startups, government regulation stands as a double-edged sword. While its primary role is to ensure safety and fairness, regulation can either stifle innovation or provide the guardrails necessary for sustainable growth. Navigating these waters requires entrepreneurs to understand the nuances of compliance and the impact it can have on their burgeoning enterprises. In a world where rapid advancements demand a delicate balance, embracing regulation doesn't mean yielding creativity; rather, it's about leveraging these rules as a framework for crafting ground-breaking solutions within a safe and ethical environment. For the startup aiming to disrupt, comprehension of the regulatory environment isn't just beneficial—it's essential. Crafting strategies that harmonize innovation with regulation can unlock potent opportunities, allowing businesses not only to thrive in today's market but to lead it into the future.

Understanding Compliance and Impact

In the delicate dance of innovation and regulation, compliance stands as a pivotal axis around which business operations must orbit. For entrepreneurs and veterans alike within the tech industry, grasping the intricate relationship between regulation and innovation is not just beneficial but necessary for survival. Government regulations represent both a guide rail and a hurdle—they can fortify markets, ensuring safety and fairness, yet also constrain the speed at which new ideas can emerge and evolve.

Compliance is about adhering to a framework of established laws and regulations. For startups venturing into the vast unknown of technology development, these laws can act as a map, outlining territories that are considered legal and safe, and those that are fraught with risks—be they ethical, financial, or legal. But for many, especially within fast-moving tech sectors like AI or blockchain, these frameworks can feel like they're lagging behind the pace of technological change, leading to a push-and-pull dynamic where innovators often find themselves skirting the edges of what's permitted.

Regulation can take many forms, including data protection laws, environmental standards, and competition policies. Each exerts a distinct influence on how businesses operate. For example, data privacy regulations like GDPR in Europe have radically redefined how companies handle personal data, offering a model for consumer protection that has echoes in legislation worldwide. Entrepreneurs operating in these environments must prioritize data compliance, often revising business models or products to align with these legal mandates. The cost of non-compliance isn't just a fine—it's the loss of consumer trust, which can be devastating in an era where data privacy is fiercely valued.

A crucial yet challenging aspect of navigating compliance is its impact on innovation. On one hand, regulations are designed to prevent monopolistic practices and protect consumer rights, fostering an environment where new players can enter the market. This can democratize innovation, allowing more voices to be heard and fresh ideas to flourish. On the other hand, excessive regulation can stymie growth, creating barriers to entry that only the well-funded can overcome, thus consolidating power within established companies that can afford the high compliance costs.

The tech industry's history is rife with examples demonstrating how compliance has shaped—and at times reshaped—tech trajectories. Take the telecommunications sector, where regulatory intervention transformed monopolies into competitive arenas, or the financial industry, where fintech disruptors have had to meticulously navigate complex regulatory waters to unseat traditional banking giants.

For startups, understanding the requirements of compliance can be especially daunting. It involves not just a legal understanding but a strategic one—knowing when to comply, when to challenge, and sometimes, when to innovate around regulation. This requires a nuanced approach, often demanding dedicated resources and continuous adaptation to stay ahead of regulatory changes, which can vary significantly from one region to another.

It's also important to consider the broader societal impact of compliance. Effective regulations can establish trust between companies and the public, ensuring that technology is developed and implemented ethically and responsibly. For instance, environmental regulations require tech companies to reduce carbon footprints, pushing them to innovate in sustainable energy use. This has spurred advancements in green technologies and propelled the industry toward a more sustainable future, aligning business growth with societal well-being.

Moreover, navigating compliance isn't just an obstacle—it's also an opportunity. Companies that successfully integrate compliance into their business strategy often enjoy a competitive advantage. They can enter new markets more swiftly, gain consumer trust, and foster collaborative relationships with regulators. This breeds a brand reputation of reliability and integrity, critical assets in competitive tech landscapes.

Interestingly, as companies scale, maintaining compliance becomes increasingly complex. What works for a startup may not suffice for a global corporation. The transition from small-scale operations to a multinational presence demands rigorous adherence to a more complex set of regulations. Here, the role of regulatory technology (regtech) becomes essential, enabling companies to automate compliance processes, minimize risks, and remain agile amidst changing laws.

However, the drive for compliance must not override the inherent value of innovation. There's a danger that overemphasis on regulatory adherence can lead companies to a risk-averse mentality, stifling creativity and discouraging bold ventures. Balancing compliance with innovation requires a forward-thinking mindset that values proactive rather than reactive strategies. Successful entrepreneurs don't just abide by regulations—they anticipate changes, influence policy discourse, and shape the regulatory environment to foster innovation.

The conversation around compliance, therefore, is not just about keeping within the permissible lines—it's about steering the course towards meaningful and impactful innovation that considers the whole ecosystem. Entrepreneurs need to engage with policymakers, understand the implications of regulations, and advocate for laws that inspire growth while safeguarding public interest. Through this engagement, they can help shape a balanced regulatory landscape where technology can thrive responsibly.

In sum, understanding compliance and its impact isn't merely a chapter in the entrepreneurial playbook; it's an ongoing narrative that each company writes through its actions, decisions, and innovations. As tech continues to advance, so too must the strategies to integrate safety and ingenuity, ensuring that regulation remains a bridge to new horizons rather than a barrier to creativity. This delicate balance holds the key to sustainable success in a world where technology is ever entwined with the rhythms of regulation.

Balancing Innovation and Safety

In the fast-paced world of technology and startups, the tension between innovation and safety is ever-present. As new products and services are developed, the pressure to push boundaries can sometimes overshadow the need for due diligence and safety measures. This tension becomes particularly palpable when considering the role of government regulation in shaping and sometimes constraining these advances. For entrepreneurs, understanding this balance is crucial not just for compliance but for long-term success.

Innovation, by its very nature, induces change and disruption. It's about thinking differently, about rejecting the status quo in pursuit of a more effective or revolutionary approach. Startups, born from this spirit, thrive on the energy of fresh ideas and the promise of what's possible. However, with this constant push for new horizons comes the question: What happens when innovations introduce risks that could impact society at large?

Navigating these waters requires a keen awareness of regulatory landscapes. Governments around the world implement regulations to protect consumers, ensure fair market practices, and prevent potential negative impacts of new technologies. Regulations can provide a framework that encourages companies to consider the wider implications of their innovations, from data privacy and security to ethical uses of technology.

Take, for example, the evolving field of artificial intelligence. The potential applications of AI are vast and transformative, but so too are the ethical dilemmas and safety concerns associated with its use. Governments and regulatory bodies face the daunting task of fostering an environment where AI development can flourish, yet remain grounded in ethical practices that protect individuals and society. Striking this balance is no small feat.

There's a historical precedent for this balancing act. The tech world has witnessed firsthand the consequences of unleashing unchecked innovation. Think back to the early days of the internet, where a flurry of rapid advancements led to the dot-com bubble and its eventual burst. This period highlighted how the race for innovation, without a parallel emphasis on safety and sustainability, could lead to economic fallout.

Yet, the presence of regulation isn't meant to stifle creativity. On the contrary, it can act as a guiding hand to ensure that innovations serve the greater good while minimizing risks. Some of the most successful tech companies have embraced regulatory challenges as opportunities to refine their products, improve safety, and earn consumer trust. Compliance becomes not just a legal obligation but a strategic advantage.

Moreover, when regulations are crafted with input from industry experts, they can accommodate the nuances of technology development while upholding safety standards. This symbiotic relationship allows both regulators and innovators to work toward common goals. Collaborative dialogue between stakeholders can lead to regulations that are flexible, scalable, and better aligned with the rapid advancements in tech.

Entrepreneurs would do well to view regulations not as obstacles but as a framework for responsible innovation. By integrating compliance into their business strategies, they not only avoid potential pitfalls but can also leverage regulation as a unique selling point. Consumers today are increasingly conscious of the ethical dimensions of the products and services they use. Demonstrating a commitment to safety and ethics can enhance brand reputation and loyalty.

However, it's essential for entrepreneurs and regulators alike to recognize that the pace of innovation often outstrips the speed at which regulations can adapt. This lag poses its own set of challenges, as outdated regulations may inadequately address the realities of new technologies. As such, proactive engagement with regulatory bodies and participation in policy discussions can help shape future guidelines that are more inclusive of emerging trends.

In this dynamic landscape, the dialogue between innovation and safety is ongoing. Entrepreneurs in the tech industry must continually reassess their approaches, ensuring that their trailblazing efforts do not inadvertently compromise safety or ethics. For those willing to embrace this dual focus, the rewards can be profound: not only in terms of business success but also in contributing positively to society.

The role of government regulation in balancing innovation with safety can be likened to a dance between creativity and responsibility. As the tech world continues to evolve, entrepreneurs are invited to lead this dance, setting a tempo that is both adventurous and conscientious, ensuring that the legacy of their innovations is one of integrity and ingenuity.

Chapter 22: Sustaining Innovation and Growth

In the ever-evolving tech landscape, sustaining innovation and growth isn't just a goal; it's a necessity for survival. Entrepreneurs and businesses alike must foster an environment where innovation thrives and growth is continuous. This involves leveraging strategies that encourage creative thinking, team collaboration, and openness to change. The challenge, however, is overcoming innovation stagnation, a common hurdle where companies risk becoming complacent. Successful businesses continuously iterate on their products, ensuring they meet market demands and set the pace for future trends. By embracing a culture of experimental learning and agile adaptation, leaders can revolutionize their strategies to unlock new pathways for growth. It's about nurturing a mindset that sees change not as a threat, but as an opportunity for advancement. This proactive approach doesn't just keep a company relevant; it propels it to the forefront of its industry, ensuring its place as a trailblazer in an ever-changing world.

Strategies for Continuous Improvement

In the dynamic world of technology and startups, resting on laurels can be a surefire path to obsolescence. Companies that lead their industries have a common trait: a relentless pursuit of continuous improvement. For entrepreneurs and established businesses alike, fostering an environment where iteration and enhancement are embedded into the company culture is critical for sustained innovation and growth.

But, what exactly does continuous improvement mean in the context of tech innovation? It's the commitment to ongoing development not just of products, but of processes, people, and perspectives. This journey requires both a macro and micro-level focus—a bird's-eye view to guide strategic direction and an attention to detail that refines day-to-day operations. Implementing continuous improvement strategies means encouraging teams to question the status quo, iterate on existing solutions, and explore uncharted territories.

Successful companies often implement **feedback loops** to fuel their iterative processes. These loops can be internal, stemming from employee insights or interdepartmental collaborations, as well as external, derived from customer reviews or market data. Take, for instance, the approach of some tech giants who regularly release beta versions of products and gather user feedback. This not only increases user engagement but also fine-tunes the product based on real-world applications, reducing the risk of releasing something that doesn't meet customer expectations.

Another key strategy for sustaining growth is the *embrace of failure* as a learning mechanism. It sounds counterintuitive, but failure is one of the most potent catalysts for improvement. In Silicon Valley's renowned culture, failure is often seen not as a defeat but as a stepping stone. Companies that understand this encourage risk-taking and see each setback as an opportunity to extract valuable insights and drive progress. By fostering a culture where employees aren't afraid to fail, businesses can propel themselves forward through their newfound learnings.

Moreover, fostering a **culture of curiosity** is essential. When employees feel empowered to question why things are done a certain way and propose alternatives, it leads to a vibrant, innovative atmosphere. Encouraging team members to stay curious and engage in lifelong learning pays dividends. Businesses can facilitate this by providing access to educational resources, hosting workshops, and supporting participation in conferences. By doing so, they invest in their workforce's growth, directly contributing to the company's capability to innovate.

Investing in *technology and tools* that enable improvement is another critical approach. The fast-paced nature of tech development demands tools that not only meet current needs but are also adaptable to the rapid changes in the tech landscape. This could mean investing in the latest project management software, adopting advanced analytics platforms for better decision-making, or leveraging AI to automate repetitive tasks. Modern tools can help streamline operations and free up employees' time, allowing them to focus on more value-driven work.

It's also important for companies to have a **clear vision** and communicate it consistently across all levels of the organization. A well-articulated vision serves as a beacon, guiding strategic improvements and allowing everyone in the company to understand how their roles contribute to the larger objectives. This creates alignment and ensures that efforts towards continuous improvement are purposeful and cohesive.

While internal mechanisms are crucial, external partnerships and *collaborations* shouldn't be overlooked as significant contributors to continuous improvement. Partnering with other firms, whether through joint ventures or consortiums, can lead to sharing best practices, gaining access to new markets, and sparking innovation by bringing in fresh, diverse perspectives. These collaborations can be particularly advantageous in tackling challenges that require interdisciplinary expertise.

On a strategic level, regularly revisiting and **evaluating processes** is indispensable. Continuous improvement necessitates a proactive stance in assessing which processes are effective and which ones need rethinking. Lean methodologies, for example, can help identify wasteful practices, allowing teams to remove inefficiencies and enhance performance. This focus on refinement can be applied across various aspects of a business, from manufacturing to customer service, ensuring every part of the operation is optimized for better outcomes.

Finally, as technology continues to advance at an unprecedented rate, leaders must remain **adaptive**. Flexibility in strategy and operations is key to navigating the perpetual waves of change in the tech industry. Organizations that cling rigidly to outdated practices find themselves outpaced by more agile competitors. A nimble approach allows companies not only to respond quickly to changes but to anticipate and lead them.

By integrating these strategies for continuous improvement, businesses position themselves not just to survive but thrive in an ever-changing landscape. The journey involves consistent effort, a willingness to learn, and a steadfast commitment to evolving. Above all, it demands a recognition that though the destination is important, it's the ongoing journey of improvement that fuels lasting innovation and growth.

Overcoming Innovation Stagnation

Innovation isn't a destination. It's a continuous journey, fraught with obstacles and detours that can easily lead to stagnation. For entrepreneurs, tech companies, and startups alike, continuing to innovate is crucial for surviving and thriving in an ever-evolving industry. The stakes are high— getting stuck in a rut can mean the difference between leading an industry and becoming obsolete.

One effective strategy to overcome innovation stagnation is to foster a culture where change is not only accepted but encouraged. Take, for example, Amazon's continuous evolution from an online bookstore to a retail giant with a diverse portfolio. This transformation didn't happen overnight but was driven by a culture that valued new ideas, risk-taking, and learning from failure. Companies that encourage experimentation see a direct impact on their ability to innovate consistently.

It's also essential to diversify perspectives within an organization. Bringing together teams with varied backgrounds—different disciplines, professional experiences, and even cultural standpoints —can lead to breakthroughs that a homogenous group might miss. This diversity of thought challenges the status quo, offering fresh angles to age-old problems and leading to often unexpected but valuable innovations.

Moreover, managing where efforts and resources are concentrated is critical. A hyper-focus on short-term profitability can stifle long-term innovation. Companies would do well to direct a certain percentage of their investments, say 70% to current business models, 20% to scouting for the next big thing, and 10% to moonshot projects. This balanced portfolio approach helps keep the innovation pipeline flowing while ensuring steady growth.

Incorporating real-time feedback from users is another tool to sidestep stagnation. Consider how software companies utilize beta testing and online forums for direct input. They use this real-world feedback to update and iterate, delivering products that meet customer needs more precisely and keeping products fresh and relevant. In today's connected world, not leveraging this direct link with the customer would be a squandered opportunity.

Partnerships and collaborations with other innovative companies can also provide a needed jolt. Shared risk and shared knowledge pools can lead to collaborative breakthroughs. A noteworthy example is Apple's and IBM's partnership, where Apple's design expertise and IBM's enterprise capabilities resulted in business-focused apps that neither company could have achieved alone.

Technology itself can assist in overcoming stagnation. Implementing cutting-edge AI and machine learning algorithms can offer insights that are otherwise difficult to glean. These technologies can predict trends, recommend innovations, and identify areas ripe for innovation, thus freeing human minds to focus on strategic thinking.

Nonetheless, the human element remains irreplaceable. Building a team that is passionate about innovation is another critical component. A dedicated innovation team is a living embodiment of a company's commitment to its innovative future. This team should have the authority and resources to make changes, take risks, and ask questions no one else dares question.

Leadership plays a pivotal role in preventing stagnation. Leaders who themselves embody a curious and open mindset inspire their teams to follow suit. They create an environment where new ideas are expected, not just welcomed. Employees have to feel safe to step outside their comfort zones and know that their ideas, no matter how unpolished initially, will be valued.

Failure, as unwelcome as it can be, should be viewed as a part of the innovation process. Learning to fail fast and fail forward helps in refining ideas and approaches quickly. This iterative process means potential solutions can be teased out faster, helping to sustain ongoing innovation.

Finally, external factors like market conditions, trends, and regulatory pressures should also be monitored. Being ahead of the curve means recognizing which changes can have significant impact and preparing adequately. Proactive steps in anticipation of these external disruptions can safeguard a company's innovative position and keep it from being derailed by unexpected market shifts.

The battle against innovation stagnation is multifaceted. It's about maintaining an organizational appetite for learning, fostering a supportive culture where ideas blossom into tangible innovations. Most importantly, it's not something that happens passively; it requires constant nurturing, evaluation, and iteration. By addressing these elements head-on, companies and entrepreneurs can ensure they remain on the cutting edge, no matter how fast the world around them might change.

Chapter 23: The Future of Work

As we venture into the future of work, it's clear that the intersection of technology and human ambition is reshaping the landscape at an unprecedented pace. Remote work, once a necessity born of global circumstance, has evolved into a cornerstone of modern business operations, demanding flexibility and adaptability. The roles and skills required today are vastly different from those of even a decade ago, with an emphasis on digital fluency, creative problem-solving, and emotional intelligence. Entrepreneurs and innovators must embrace these shifts, fostering environments that prioritize both technological advancements and the human elements of empathy and collaboration. The future belongs to those who can navigate this dynamic interplay, where traditional career paths are becoming as fluid as the technologies that drive them, and the spirit of entrepreneurship is vital in developing innovative solutions to meet the challenges and opportunities ahead.

Remote Work and the Tech Industry

Remote work has transformed from a perk to a necessity in the tech industry in recent years. The landscape of work itself has undergone a seismic shift, accelerated by technological advancements and societal changes. Pandemic-induced home offices have given way to long-term remote work policies, as businesses and employees recognize the benefits that flexibility and technological empowerment bring. What once seemed like futuristic speculation is now an integrated element of how tech companies operate.

At the heart of this remote work revolution is technology—both as an enabler and a beneficiary. Historically, tech companies were among the first to adopt remote work due to their inherent knack for innovation and digital-native orientation. High-speed internet, video conferencing, cloud services, and project management tools have provided the backbone for remote work. Consider the role of platforms like Zoom, Microsoft Teams, and Slack, which became essential tools almost overnight, propelling firms into a new era of digital collaboration. The rapid evolution and adoption of these tools were as much about survival as they were about embracing opportunity.

Yet, this trend is not without challenges. Companies have had to experiment with new management styles that accommodate a dispersed workforce. How do you foster company culture when team members are spread across the globe? Managers today must cultivate trust and independence while balancing accountability, a task that can be complex but not insurmountable. Many companies have implemented regular virtual check-ins, digital team-building activities, and flexible work hours to maintain cohesion and morale.

For entrepreneurs and those interested in startup culture, embracing remote work doesn't just mean letting employees work from home. It means rethinking traditional business operations and focusing on outcomes rather than processes. It promises greater access to a global talent pool and the ability to collaborate across borders without geographical constraints. In a sense, the office of the future is now more a concept than a physical location. The tech industry, ever an exemplar of adaptability, offers a blueprint for businesses in other sectors to follow.

The financial implications are also significant. Companies cutting costs by reducing office space have found themselves in a scenario to reallocate funds towards employee enrichment and technological investments. There are also economic benefits for employees, such as reduced commute times and associated costs. This democratization of workplace geography can lead to a more balanced professional life, allowing individuals to tailor their work environments to suit their personal needs.

Looking forward, this shift continues to produce consequences that ripple through corporate hierarchies and societal norms alike. We've seen the dawn of a meritocratic and results-driven work culture, where skills and productivity count more than time spent in an office chair. As companies move forward, many grapple with the question of how to balance remote work with potential desires for in-person interaction, leading to innovative hybrid models tailored to diversify workplace needs.

From a talent perspective, the rise of remote work has shifted the paradigm of employee expectations. Candidates now often prioritize flexible work arrangements as much as salary or career growth opportunities. Companies failing to provide such flexibility risk alienating top talent and lagging in the competitive tech industry landscape. Simultaneously, opportunities open up for those in less traditional tech hubs, helping to decentralize the concentration of tech talent away from locations like Silicon Valley.

It's also vital to consider the broader implications of remote work on innovation within the tech sector. While water cooler conversations and spontaneous brainstorming sessions historically sparked bright ideas, remote work pushes teams to find new ways to innovate. The challenge lies in ensuring robust communication channels and fostering collaboration, which, when done correctly, can span distances and time zones.

Leaders have a unique role in paving the way for this new era of work. Visionary figures in the tech sphere are often those who approach transformation with both optimism and realism, paving a path that looks beyond immediate gains to long-term value creation. As such, the evolution of work will likely become a key focus of leadership development, shaping the strategic thinking of the next generation of tech leaders.

It's an exciting, albeit uncertain, time. The path is not without its hurdles and learning curves, but the potential for transformation in how we work is both inspiring and daunting. Remote work offers a proposition where business can thrive not in spite of geographical distance but because of it, promising a future where work is more inclusive, efficient, and equitable.

In conclusion, the tech industry is at the forefront once again, redefining what work can be in the years to come. The transition to remote work in this sector spotlights the dynamic nature of entrepreneurship and innovation. For those willing to adapt, these changes bring unprecedented opportunities for growth, efficiency, and disruption—key tenets of success in the fast-paced world of tech startups. Remote work isn't just a trend; it's the ground on which future tech companies will build their empires.

Skills and Roles of Tomorrow

The future of work is a fascinating puzzle, intricately woven with threads of technology, innovation, and human ingenuity. To grasp the full spectrum of skills and roles that tomorrow's economy will demand, we must first understand how technology is reshaping the work landscape. As automation, artificial intelligence, and digital communication break traditional barriers, the roles we see are evolving at an unprecedented pace.

Most notably, with automation taking over repetitive tasks, skills centered around human ingenuity have never been more critical. Employers are valuing creative thinkers, problem-solvers, and innovators who can leverage technology in unique ways. The importance of soft skills like empathy, communication, and adaptability is rising rapidly, suggesting that our future workplaces will require a balance between technical prowess and emotional intelligence.

Let's unravel the specific roles that are poised to take center stage. Consider, for instance, the role of data scientists and analysts. These individuals not only interpret vast amounts of data but also extract meaningful insights that drive strategic business decisions. Their ability to translate raw data into actionable intelligence will be indispensable as companies strive to maintain competitive edges.

Then there's the surge in demand for cybersecurity experts. With increasing cyber threats, this role isn't just about prevention; it's about innovation. Cybersecurity experts will need to anticipate potential threats and develop cutting-edge solutions to protect sensitive information. Their work ensures the safety and integrity of digital landscapes, making them indispensable to any tech-savvy organization.

Moreover, roles like AI specialists and machine learning engineers are becoming integral. These experts create systems that learn and adapt over time, automating complex processes and generating efficiencies. As AI technology becomes more advanced, these roles will continue to evolve, requiring a mix of deep technical expertise and creative application of AI solutions.

The rise of remote work arrangements brings another layer to this evolving tapestry. With geographical boundaries blurring, the skills required to manage remote teams effectively are gaining prominence. Project managers, communication specialists, and leaders proficient in digital collaboration tools are becoming key players in ensuring that teams operate efficiently, regardless of location.

New educational modules are emerging to cater to these shifts. Curricula are increasingly focused on interdisciplinary studies, combining programming with philosophy, or engineering with design. This approach reflects a growing understanding that tomorrow's leaders will need to draw from diverse fields to solve complex challenges.

Entrepreneurs and startups, in particular, are driving demand for hybrid skills. In this environment, employees are expected to juggle multiple roles, necessitating a diverse skill set that spans various disciplines. This shift is fostering an entrepreneurial mindset across industries, encouraging individuals to be innovative, adaptable, and proactive.

Furthermore, environmental sustainability is pushing new roles into the limelight. Sustainability consultants, renewable energy experts, and green tech innovators are becoming crucial as companies aim to reduce their carbon footprints. These roles require not only technical knowledge but also an understanding of environmental policies and consumer expectations.

As we look towards a future shaped by continuous change, lifelong learning becomes a cornerstone of career development. The ability to learn, unlearn, and relearn new skills will distinguish those who thrive from those who merely survive. Online courses, digital certifications, and experiential learning sessions are becoming the norm, facilitating educational growth outside traditional contexts.

In this evolving landscape, one must also acknowledge the role of technology itself in creating new teaching methods. Virtual reality (VR) and augmented reality (AR) are revolutionizing training programs, offering immersive experiences that enhance understanding and retention of complex concepts.

Finally, the emphasis on ethical considerations cannot be overlooked. As AI and automation increasingly influence decision-making processes, ethical AI developers and ethicists will play crucial roles in ensuring fair and just applications of these technologies. Their work helps align technological progress with societal values, maintaining a human-centric focus amidst digital transformation.

In summary, the skills and roles of tomorrow are a tapestry woven with technical brilliance and soulful humanity. As we stand on the brink of this new era, it's clear that success will belong to those who adapt, innovate, and embrace continuous learning. Whether you're an aspiring entrepreneur or a tech enthusiast, understanding and preparing for this shift will be key to thriving in the dynamic future of work.

Chapter 24: Lessons for Aspiring Entrepreneurs

In the ever-evolving landscape of technology and innovation, aspiring entrepreneurs must learn from the triumphs and trials of those who've pioneered before them. Successful founders often share a common thread —resilience in the face of failure and a keen understanding of when to pivot and when to persist. To navigate this complex journey, it's crucial to embrace adaptability, align your vision with market demands, and maintain an unwavering commitment to your core values. Many entrepreneurs stumble on the path of rapid scalability, underestimating the significance of a robust team and culture. Equally, some falter by neglecting customer feedback, which is invaluable for refining products and services. Ultimately, the key to startup success lies in balancing risk with opportunity, fostering a culture of creativity and perseverance, and continuously learning from both past missteps and meaningful successes.

Insights from Successful Founders

In the world of startups and tech innovation, much is learned from those who've blazed the trail before us. Successful founders often possess a unique blend of vision, resilience, and adaptability that sets them apart. They aren't just pioneers of technology; they're sculptors of culture and shapers of tomorrow. Their insights not only illuminate the path for aspiring entrepreneurs but also offer timeless lessons in leadership and innovation.

One thread common among many successful founders is their profound clarity of vision. Steve Jobs, for instance, was known for his ability to see not only what the market demanded today but what it would require tomorrow. He didn't merely want to make computers; he wanted to transform how people interact with technology. This kind of foresight is vital. It requires not just understanding technology but grasping human behavior and anticipating shifts in consumer expectation. For entrepreneurs, cultivating a clear vision that aligns with future trends can be the distinguishing factor between success and obscurity.

Moreover, there's an inherent resilience that defines these founders. Starting a company, particularly in the tech sector, is rife with challenges —technological hurdles, financial constraints, and competitive pressures among them. Jeff Bezos faced skepticism and financial challenges in Amazon's early days, yet his resilience and unwavering belief in the internet's retail potential carried him forward. His journey underscores the necessity of perseverance, especially when confronting setbacks that at first seem insurmountable.

Adaptability is another key trait found in successful founders. In the fast-paced tech environment, flexibility is akin to survival. Mark Zuckerberg's ability to navigate the evolving landscape of social media and digital communication exemplifies the importance of staying pliable. Facebook's pivot from a college networking site to a global platform highlights how adaptability can lead to expansive growth. Entrepreneurs today must be prepared to pivot quickly, respond to market feedback, and not wed themselves to a single path if circumstances shift.

While vision, resilience, and adaptability form the cornerstone of entrepreneurial success, collaboration plays a critical role too. The narrative of collaborative innovation is especially evident in companies like Google, where the exchange of ideas fuels technological advancement. Larry Page and Sergey Brin leveraged their partnership to create a company greater than the sum of its parts, showing that fostering a culture of collaboration can propel a startup's vision further than individual effort alone. Aspiring entrepreneurs should seek to build teams that echo this dynamic of shared success.

Another crucial insight from successful founders is the importance of understanding one's customer deeply. Many tech founders talk about the "voice of the customer" being an integral factor in their product development. Airbnb was born from a profound understanding of the gap in the hospitality market and recognizing what travelers truly valued—a personalized experience that big hotels could not offer. This knowledge propelled them to innovate continually, ensuring that their offerings stayed relevant.

Successful founders also emphasize the importance of maintaining a strong company culture. Culture isn't just about perks or office aesthetics; it's about shared values and mission-focused work. When Elon Musk discusses his ventures at Tesla or SpaceX, he often cites culture and mission alignment as central to overcoming challenges and driving innovation. For startups, instilling a strong culture from the outset can serve as a glue that holds the team together, especially through challenging times.

Furthermore, mentorship and learning are often valued highly by founders. Many successful entrepreneurs attribute their growth to guidance received from mentors who once faced similar struggles. Having access to experienced voices offers fresh perspectives and can help in navigating complex decisions. As tech landscapes evolve, continuous learning—both from mentors and through self-directed study —remains indispensable.

A consistent theme also surfaces around taking calculated risks. Founders who succeed in sprawling tech ventures often advocate for a balanced approach to risk. Elon Musk, for example, is known for his bold, audacious ventures. Yet underlying these are meticulous calculations and informed speculation. Startups must be willing to take risks to innovate yet do so with the calculated optimism that balances vision with reality.

Financial acumen is another crucial lesson. Managing resources efficiently while scaling quickly is a delicate balance that's often challenging yet essential for enduring success. Many founders recommend prioritizing sustainable growth over rapid, unsustainable expansion. Founders like Warren Buffet emphasize frugality and understanding financial intricacies as pivotal elements that help in steering a young company through economic uncertainties.

Lastly, many successful founders convey the importance of embracing failure as a learning tool. Failure isn't just an outcome; it's a step in the iterative process of becoming better. The stories of entrepreneurs like Thomas Edison reveal that failures are often precursors to monumental successes, offering lessons that refine a product or strategy. Aspiring entrepreneurs should adopt a mindset where failure is part of the journey, fostering a culture of learning and adaptability.

In sum, insights from successful founders offer a treasure trove of wisdom. They teach us not only about technology and innovation but also about the human elements of leadership, vision, and sustenance. These lessons guide aspiring entrepreneurs in crafting their own narratives of success, attuning them to the rhythms of industry evolution and personal growth.

Common Pitfalls and How to Avoid Them

Embarking on the entrepreneurial journey is much like setting sail on uncharted waters. The thrill of the unknown is matched only by the risk of missteps, which can be daunting for even the most seasoned explorers. In the fast-paced world of tech startups, where the stakes are high and the margins for error are low, understanding common pitfalls can be a game-changer. Let's explore these hazards and how to steer clear of them.

One of the most pervasive risks entrepreneurs face is **ignoring the voice of the customer**. It's ironic, isn't it? In a world hyper-focused on innovation, it's easy to forget that the end goal is solving real-world problems for real people. When founders become too absorbed in the allure of their own technology, they risk losing touch with the very market they wish to captivate. The solution? Cultivate an open feedback loop with your customer base. Regularly solicit honest opinions and adapt your product or service to meet evolving needs. By doing so, you'll forge a stronger connection with your audience and refine your offering to provide true value.

Another trap that ensnares many is the **underestimation of financial management**. It's one thing to secure funding; it's entirely another to manage it wisely. Misallocating resources or failing to plan for leaner times can quickly derail a promising startup. Entrepreneurs should learn to balance visionary spending with prudent fiscal strategies. Ensure you have a detailed budget, maintain a healthy cash flow, and prepare for the unexpected with a robust financial cushion. Vigilant financial oversight isn't merely a safeguard—it's a catalyst for sustained growth.

One could argue that the tech industry is synonymous with **rapid change**. This environment fosters tremendous opportunities but also poses the risk of obsolescence. Startups that fail to adapt can quickly become relics. The antidote is a culture of continuous learning and agility. Encourage your team to stay abreast of technological trends, and don't be afraid to pivot when necessary. Remaining rigid in your approach is a surefire way to stagnation, while embracing change can lead to innovation breakthroughs.

Many entrepreneurs mistakenly equate **speed with success**. The startup mythos often glamorizes fast growth and overnight successes, but in reality, scaling too quickly can be a double-edged sword. Rapid expansion without the requisite infrastructure can lead to quality control issues, customer dissatisfaction, and burnout. Instead, focus on building a scalable model that can handle growth without compromising core values or service standards. It's often the tortoise, not the hare, that eventually wins the race.

Furthermore, **founder dynamics can be a silent startup killer**. Partnerships based on friendship or convenience rather than complementary skills and aligned vision can falter under pressure. It's essential to choose co-founders who not only augment your strengths but also share your dedication to the venture's mission. Open communication, clear role definitions, and mutual respect are the bedrock of successful collaborations.

Let's not overlook the temptation of the **"shiny object syndrome."** In an industry rife with groundbreaking developments, it's all too easy to become distracted by the latest trends or technologies. Chasing every new opportunity without a clear strategic focus can dilute your efforts and lead to a loss of direction. Entrepreneurs should establish a clear vision, prioritize initiatives, and say "no" to opportunities that don't align with their long-term goals. Discipline in decision-making will keep your startup focused and driven.

Additionally, **neglecting company culture** can have severe, although sometimes subtle, repercussions. A toxic work environment undermines innovation and productivity, resulting in high employee turnover and poor performance. As founders, it's crucial to deliberately shape a positive culture that embodies your values and attracts talent. Cultivating an inclusive and supportive environment not only boosts morale but also encourages creativity and loyalty.

The final pitfall to consider is the **over-reliance on venture capital**. While venture capital can provide the fuel needed to scale a startup rapidly, over-dependence can diminish a founder's control over their company's destiny. It can also pressure startups into chasing unsustainable growth metrics. Entrepreneurs should explore alternative funding sources, like bootstrapping or angel investors, to maintain greater autonomy and develop a more sustainable growth model.

Learning from these common pitfalls and their solutions can make the difference between failure and success for aspiring entrepreneurs. While the path of entrepreneurship is fraught with challenges, being aware of and prepared for these obstacles is essential. By maintaining focus on customer needs, managing finances wisely, staying adaptable, pacing growth, nurturing founder dynamics, averting distractions, building a positive culture, and balancing funding sources, startups can navigate these treacherous waters more deftly. As you chart your course, remember that these insights are your compass, allowing you not only to survive but to thrive amidst adversity.

Chapter 25: Case Studies of Noteworthy Failures

In the vibrant tapestry of tech entrepreneurship, the stories of triumph are often interwoven with threads of failure. Some of the most illuminating lessons come from scrutinizing high-profile collapses within the industry. Take, for instance, the dramatic fall of WeWork, which, at its peak, was valorized as a beacon of modern entrepreneurial spirit yet unraveled under unsustainable business practices and leadership flaws. Similarly, Theranos captivated the world with its promise to revolutionize healthcare but stumbled due to a lack of transparency and overreliance on unproven technology. These case studies, while stark in their endings, serve a crucial role in the entrepreneurial ecosystem—reminding us that unchecked ambition, without a foundation of integrity and adaptability, can lead even the mightiest ventures to ruin. By understanding the dynamics of these failures, budding entrepreneurs can better navigate the turbulent waters of the startup world, not just envisioning success but ensuring it through rigorous planning and ethical leadership.

Analyzing High-Profile Collapses

In the tech industry, renowned for its groundbreaking innovations and rapid growth, the specter of failure looms large. The annals of Silicon Valley are punctuated by stories of high-profile collapses, each carrying its own narrative of ambition, misstep, and consequence. Understanding these collapses involves peeling back layers of complexity to reveal why some ventures, often brimming with potential and backed by immense resources, ultimately unravel. Analyzing these cases offers invaluable insights for entrepreneurs and business leaders aiming to avoid similar fates.

At the heart of many monumental failures is a tendency to assume that growth and success are infinitely sustainable. Many startups scale aggressively, encouraged by a market that seems boundless, only to realize that their foundations are not as robust as presumed. Take for example, a notable case from the early 2000s when unchecked exuberance and speculative investments fueled myriad dot-com startups. As the bubble burst, it became glaringly evident that many of these companies lacked sustainable business models and were overly reliant on speculative capital.

Corporate governance is another pivotal element in understanding these failures. Time and again, the absence of strong oversight and accountability has paved the way for catastrophic misjudgments. The infamous case of Enron serves as a chilling reminder of how internal failings in transparency and accountability can culminate in one of the biggest corporate scandals, leading to a spectacular collapse. More than just financial malpractices, it was a failure of leadership and ethics that imploded what was once a market darling.

Moreover, considering the speed with which technology evolves, companies that fail to adapt often find themselves left in the dust. Kodak, once a titan in the photography world, serves as a cautionary tale of what happens when adaptation falls short. Even though they developed digital photography technology first, their hesitance to cannibalize their profitable film business allowed competitors to seize market dominance. This reluctance to innovate from within illustrates how even industry leaders can stumble when they don't embrace the disruptive technologies they've pioneered.

In parallel, one must examine how ignorance of market signals can exacerbate other issues. Blackberry's downfall, for example, wasn't merely because of its failure to innovate like Kodak, but also its inability to interpret consumer demands as the smartphone market fundamentally shifted. While iPhones and Android devices quickly pivoted to touchscreen interfaces, Blackberry clung to its physical keyboard, a decision that alienated a massive customer base. Ignoring or misreading customer preferences can turn what once seemed a niche strength into a glaring liability.

Another running theme through these collapses is the disruption of balance between innovation and operational execution. Startups, fueled by the desire to introduce new technologies at breakneck speed, often neglect the structural robustness required for sustained growth. The case of Theranos epitomizes this imbalance. Its ambition to revolutionize blood testing with minimal samples overlooked the need for solid scientific validation and systematic implementation, resulting in a downfall when reality did not meet promises.

Financial management and cash flow also play critical roles. Often, startups, boosted by impressive rounds of funding, fall into the trap of excessive spending without a clear path to profitability. WeWork, once heralded as a beacon of the sharing economy, fell victim to this very pattern. Over-leveraging resources to expand aggressively, the company ignored signs of financial instability, ultimately leading to a valuation collapse when investor confidence waned. The story of WeWork underscores the need for financial prudence even in times of flush capital.

The role of culture, too, cannot be overlooked. Several high-profile failures have their roots in toxic or dysfunctional company cultures that stymied creativity and agile decision-making. Uber, for instance, faced numerous challenges rooted in a culture that prioritized rapid growth over ethical considerations. This resulted in not just internal turmoil but also damage to its public image, necessitating significant cultural and operational overhauls to regain its footing.

As technology firms grapple with these potential pitfalls, it's essential to distill lessons from these high-profile collapses. A recurrent lesson is the importance of foresight and a measured approach to growth. Building resilient business models that incorporate rigorous financial planning, active market engagement, and a robust governance structure can create a buffer against potential disruptions.

For aspiring entrepreneurs and existing business leaders, the resounding takeaway from these stories is the need for a balanced approach to innovation and execution. It's not merely the brilliance of an idea but its practical realization and long-term sustainability that predicates success. Business is often a dance between bold vision and calculated risk, and lessons from past collapses drive home the importance of maintaining this equilibrium.

High-profile collapses also serve as a reminder of the transient nature of market leadership. They underline that success in the tech world requires continuous learning, adaptation, and humility. Companies that become complacent, or assume past success warrants future triumphs, are those most susceptible to disruptive forces.

In closing, analyzing these collapses with a discerning eye reveals patterns and practices that can either herald the downfall or the resurgence of a company. As we look forward, entrepreneurs equipped with an understanding of these tales of caution can forge paths that not only innovate but endure. The strains and stresses of the tech world are undeniable, but so too are its possibilities—for those who learn from the past and boldly navigate the future with resilience and insight.

Extracting Lessons for Future Success

Failure, often romanticized as a stepping stone to success, carries invaluable lessons for individuals willing to learn from its harsh realities. In the chaotic yet ever-inspiring world of startups, the stories of companies that have stumbled, floundered, or frankly crashed and burned are more than just cautionary tales. They're treasure troves of insight. These past failures offer roadmaps, albeit drawn in reverse, that provide nuanced guidance on what to avoid, how to pivot, and where to dig deeper when building a resilient enterprise.

Whenever a startup collapses, the gaping hole it leaves behind reveals patterns that are remarkably consistent across diverse sectors. A recurring theme is the overemphasis on speed. While the startup culture romanticizes rapid scaling, good things don't always come to those who rush. The downfall of many a fledgling enterprise has stemmed from a premature push towards growth before solidifying core products or thoroughly understanding the market landscape. In hindsight, fast growth without foundational stability can be likened to building a skyscraper on sand. Entrepreneurs must learn to balance speed with sustainability, ensuring that each growth step is firmly grounded in market realities and product feasibility.

Yet, perhaps the most instructive lesson lies in the intricate web of consumer needs vs. product features. Countless startups have developed groundbreaking technologies only to fall into the trap of assuming they know their consumer better than the consumer knows themselves. Living by the mantra "if you build it, they will come" has derailed many promising ventures. History teaches us that understanding consumer behavior and actual needs is not just a preliminary task but an ongoing commitment. This commitment requires remaining agile and open to evolving demands, ensuring that the product roadmap aligns with real, not assumed, market demands.

From these observations, it's clear that a crucial element is the ability to pivot. Take a wrong turn? Pivoting doesn't have to mean conceding defeat

—it's about adjusting approach and focus, and sometimes letting go of ego-driven persistence. This adaptability has saved many from a definitive crash, transforming potential debacles into new avenues for success. The viability of both Twitter and Slack today can be attributed to their founders' willingness to embrace drastic changes in direction when their original plans didn't pan out.

Financial mismanagement is another theme that echoes throughout the halls of startup failures. There's a persistent allure of high valuations and lucrative funding rounds, but these financial maneuvers often overshadow prudent fiscal management. Cash flow complications can overshadow even the most innovative products. Founders should remember that raising funds isn't just about accumulating resources; it's also about understanding how to manage those resources effectively—ensuring finances are directly correlated with strategic goals.

Cultivating resilient company culture is another vital lesson. Companies falter not just because of flawed products or strategies, but also due to internal discord and lack of alignment on core values. A fragmented team can't withstand external pressures or critical junctures in their journey. Fostering a culture that resonates deeply with the mission can provide scaffolding strong enough to weather even turbulent times. Leaders should invest in building collaborative environments where each team member feels part of a shared vision.

Moreover, understanding the competitive landscape is critical. Underestimating or ignoring competition has spelled the end for startups blinded by confidence in their uniqueness. It's crucial to continuously monitor competitors and acknowledge them as potential teachers rather than mere threats. Competition has a way of pushing companies to innovate beyond their comfort zones. It's a stark reminder that complacency is often the harbinger of failure.

Another key takeaway from these failure narratives is the importance of transparent, open communication. In times of crisis and uncertainty, clear communication lines between founders, employees, investors, and even customers can help mitigate damage. Open dialogues can foster collective problem-solving and instill a sense of unity during turbulent periods.

Silence, on the other hand, can breed mistrust and continuously widen existing gaps in stakeholder relations.

While technology continues to evolve at breakneck speed, regulatory environments often struggle to keep pace, and legal obstacles can trip even savvy entrepreneurs. Ignoring the regulatory landscape or approaching it with a cavalier attitude can doom visionary projects. A lesson learned here is the need for strategic foresight in compliance—a thorough understanding of the relevant legal frameworks can be the difference between revolutionary success and catastrophic failure.

The stories of failure also teach that perseverance, in its most genuine form, is essential but should be guided by informed decision-making rather than stubbornness. Herein lies the value of mentorship and advisory networks. Experienced mentors provide grounded perspectives, helping entrepreneurs differentiate between when to persist and when adaptation is necessary. They provide checks and balances, a sounding board for decisions that could make or break an enterprise.

Finally, reflecting on past failures reinforces the necessity of continuous learning and evolution. Staying tethered to a rigid business model or outdated methods can be counterproductive in a domain characterized by rapid change. Organizations committed to learning and experimentation are often those that ultimately lead their sectors. They regard mistakes as opportunities to iterate and refine, steering towards new opportunities with the conviction of experience. Embracing failure as a component of growth, they transform setbacks into setups for future triumphs.

In conclusion, while there's no formulaic blueprint to guarantee startup success, examining noteworthy failures provides a compelling narrative —a narrative filled with caution, adaptation, and perseverance. By internalizing these hard-wrought lessons, burgeoning entrepreneurs can better navigate the treacherous journey of building and scaling their ventures, using the wisdom of previous generations to illuminate their path forward.

Conclusion

The journey through the tech industry's vast landscape reveals many lessons, triumphs, and challenges. As we wrap up this exploration, it's clear that the world of startups and technology is more than just a realm of explosive growth and innovation; it's a reflection of human ambition, adaptability, and vision. Entrepreneurs and innovators have forged paths through uncharted territories, shaping the future in ways few could have anticipated.

One of the central themes that emerged is the necessity of resilience. The stories of iconic companies and leaders show that the path to success is seldom straight. From the tumultuous swings of the dot-com boom and bust to the reinvention during economic downturns, those who endure are often those who learn to navigate uncertainty with agility and tenacity. The tech industry's history teaches us that adaptability isn't just an advantage; it's a prerequisite for survival.

Moreover, innovation's lifeblood lies in its culture. Whether described as the "garage band mentality" or the push to foster creativity and disruption, the culture within tech companies plays a crucial role in their success or failure. Startups that thrive are often those that cultivate an environment where ideas can flourish, encouraging risk-taking and accepting failures as stepping stones towards breakthroughs. Steve Jobs' Apple, Google's vision for organizing the world's information, or Amazon's relentless focus on customer convenience exemplify how culture shapes the trajectory of technological progress.

Further underlining the narrative is the significant role of leadership and vision in driving companies to new heights. Entrepreneurs who lead with foresight, empathy, and decisiveness are the architects of tomorrow. They guide their teams through uncertainty, inspire loyalty, and often reimagine what is possible. The stories from Silicon Valley and beyond remind us that while technology evolves, the core of effective leadership remains steadfast: it's about unlocking potential and being prepared to question the status quo.

In today's interconnected world, these lessons are not confined to the tech industry alone. The teachings from pioneering tech companies have permeable boundaries, impacting various sectors and echoing the importance of fostering innovation, learning from failure, embracing change, and cultivating a strong company culture. These elements are universal in their application and crucial for the growth of any enterprise striving for sustainability and success.

Yet, as the industry forges ahead, it must continuously reflect on its broader implications. The rise of artificial intelligence, the ethical challenges presented by data privacy, and the responsibility of tech giants as stewards of vast amounts of information are challenges that accompany modern technology's rapid pace. It's an ongoing dialogue between progress and prudence, between opportunity and consequence.

Looking to the future, aspiring entrepreneurs and those embedded in the tech ecosystem must remain vigilant about these balances. The stories told and the insights gathered should serve as a compass, guiding the next wave of innovation and entrepreneurship towards sustainable and responsible growth. In this evolving landscape, success doesn't merely hinge on technological breakthroughs but also on the capacity to anticipate and adapt to the ethical, societal, and economic shifts that accompany technological advancement.

The tech industry, therefore, emerges not just as a driver of economic prosperity and lifestyle change but as a mirror reflecting broader societal dynamics. From diversity's vital role in innovation to the importance of aligning company culture with long-term objectives, the broader narrative underscores a profound truth: technology, while complex in its development, remains a fundamentally human endeavor.

As we conclude this exploration, it's evident that the industry's history is not just written by the successes that adorn its headlines but by the failures that shape its foundations and the lessons that propel it forward. Entrepreneurs poised on the cusp of the next significant innovation should heed these narratives. They should remember that each misstep is a lesson, each innovation is an opportunity, and each company aspires not just to break ground but to change the world.

In these stories of innovation and entrepreneurship lies a powerful invitation. It's an invitation to create, to disrupt, to inspire, and to be inspired. As the tech industry continues to evolve at a dizzying pace, may this narrative serve as a lodestar—a guiding light toward a future that honors its past, fulfills its present potential, and eagerly anticipates the horizons of tomorrow.

Appendix A: Appendix

This appendix aims to enrich our understanding of the intricate components that weave the tapestry of startup success, offering supplementary material that complements the chapters explored in this book. As we journey through these additional insights, we're reminded of the intricate balance between innovation and persistence, risk and reward, that defines entrepreneurial endeavors.

Historical Contexts and Their Influence

The historical backdrop of startups often paints a vivid picture of how an era's unique circumstances can shape industry trends and individual company trajectories. While the main chapters have touched upon key historical moments, this appendix offers glimpses of lesser-known narratives that influence modern startup culture. From unsung pioneers who laid the groundwork for technological giants to fleeting innovations that sparked revolutionary ideas, these glimpses offer invaluable lessons.

Statistical Perspectives

Diving into statistics and trends can provide a clear-eyed view of the tech startup landscape. This section presents charts and data not extensively covered earlier, shedding light on emerging markets, investment patterns, and growth metrics. Understanding these numbers not only assists in making informed strategic decisions but also highlights the potential and volatility inherent in tech entrepreneurship.

Additional Resources

- Key Books and Articles: A curated list of recommended readings that delve deeper into subjects like leadership in tech, startup ecosystems, and the philosophy of innovation.

- Online Platforms and Communities: Explore influential online spaces where entrepreneurs and tech enthusiasts congregate to share ideas, challenges, and solutions.

Future Considerations

As technology and society evolve, so too will the challenges and opportunities facing startups. This appendix extends a forward-looking glance at nascent technologies, market dynamics, and societal shifts poised to redefine the landscape. Equipped with these insights, future entrepreneurs can strategize for resilience and adaptability.

In conclusion, while the chapters of this book construct a rich narrative of the startup world through strategic analysis and storytelling, this appendix enhances our comprehensive view, offering essential details and perspectives that drive the tech industry's pulse.